"I have examined and

BOOK OF ALCOHOLICS

opening up new treasures of th

than a mere index - as a concordance, it groups words and ideas in a way which should greatly facilitate study of the book. The concordance will be an invaluable tool for deeper research into the message of A.A."

James E. Royce, S.J., Ph.D.

Professor of Alcohol Studies Seattle University, Seattle, WA., a director of the National Council on Alcoholism and author of: Alcohol Problems and Alcoholism: a Comprehensive Survey, 1981.

"It is the function of this work, **A REFERENCE GUIDE TO THE BIG BOOK OF ALCOHOLICS ANONYMOUS,** to be an excellent and thorough concordance for all those who wish to study the Big Book with diligence. It will save endless hours of searching, stop arguments before they become hardened and it will get people to the meat of what they want and need to discuss together.

This Reference Guide breaks beyond these benefits. It will put the thoughtful searcher onto parallels of words and themes, onto associations of ideas, onto repetitions of major concepts that would almost never get noticed otherwise.

An endlessly fascinating new approach to reading the Big Book, this Reference Guide will provide both enjoyment and benefit to all who seek information for sobriety and serenity."

The Rev. Bruce Van Blair
Mercer Island, WA.

How many times have you heard: "As it says in the Big Book"? AA members are constantly referring to parts, passages and pages of the Big Book of Alcoholics Anonymous. But 'exactly' where do you find these references?

A Northwest author Stewart C. has spent four years doing extensive research and referencing in compiling the "Reference Guide to the Big Book of Alcoholics Anonymous". He has taken every subject, every key phrase, concept and quotation, and created a very useful index for anyone interested in a more thorough understanding of the heart and soul of AA.

The Reference Guide to the Big Book is an excellent guide to the study of the Big Book, as well as a reference guide to its contents. It's a must for leaders of Big Book Study Groups, as well as counselors in treatment centers who teach the fundamental concepts of Alcoholics Anonymous. The reader will be able to quickly and accurately find an exact word, quotation, phrase or idea contained in the Big Book. It even has a special section on People, Places and Things.

It can also put to rest various philosophical debates such as the use of 'Recovering' vs. 'Recovered'. A quick check of the Reference Guide to the Big Book reveals that 'Recovered' is used a total of ten times: on the title page, plus pages xiii, xxiii, 17, 20, 90, 96, 132, 133 and 146. The term 'Recovering' is only used once! It's on page 122.

"As it says in the Big Book..."

Neil Scott,
Managing Editor
Alcoholism & Addiction Magazine
Seattle, WA

A REFERENCE GUIDE

TO THE BIG BOOK
OF ALCOHOLICS ANONYMOUS

Glen Abbey Books, Inc.
P.O. Box 31329
Seattle, Washington 98103

First Edition
Fourth Printing 1989
ISBN 0-934125-01-5
Published in the United States of America

A Recovery Press Book
Published by arrangement with
Glen Abbey Books, Inc.

TABLE OF CONTENTS

Page

PREFACE i
ACKNOWLEDGEMENTS ii

SECTION 1: A CONCORDANCE

Introduction iv
A Concordance 1
Appendix 1: The Disease Model 103
Appendix 2: I'll do Anything 105
Appendix 3: Man on the Bed 106
Appendix 4: Must 107
Appendix 5: Off the Beam/On the Beam 111
Appendix 6: The Promises 113
Appendix 7: God and Pronouns for God 115

SECTION 11: MOTTOES, SLOGANS & TERMS

Introduction 118
Earlier Editions 119
Mottoes, Slogans & Terms 120

SECTION 111: A GUIDE

Changes to the Big Book 126
Emphasis 130
Variants 131
People, Places and Things 132

LIST OF SYMBOLS AND ABBREVIATIONS

App.	=	an abbreviation of the word "Appendix"
ed.	=	an abbreviation of the word "edition"
f	=	a footnote in the book: Alcoholics Anonymous
ffdc	=	a notation for the front flap of the dust cover (or dust jacket)
n	=	a footnote in the book: A Reference Guide
ppt	=	an abbreviation of the expression "people, places and things"
pr.	=	an abbreviation of the word "printing"
Sect.	=	an abbreviation of the word "section"
tp	=	an abbreviation of the term "title page"

ACKNOWLEDGEMENTS

This project was made possible as a result of a collaboration between author and publisher, and so it has proved to be. To all the members of the Fellowship who shared their time and experience, I owe a debt of gratitude. I am also indebted to all the people listed below who gave their support, dedication, and enthusiasm toward the completion of this work. I am pleased to share this page with them.

S.H.C.
Seattle, Wa.
Nov. 1986

ADVISORS: John S. and Bill R.

EDITOR: Ciarán O'Mahony

COORDINATOR: Patrick M.

EDITORIAL ASST'S.: Annie M., and Jud B.

ENCOURAGEMENT: Don D., Nancy J.

Appreciation is due to the archivist of the Episcopal Diocese Of Ohio and the Akron Regional Development Board of Akron, Ohio for their contributions. I also wish to express my appreciation of the excellent research facilities and to the helpful personnel at the University of Washington (Seattle) library system and the Seattle Public Library system.

PREFACE

This Reference Guide evolved from a need for a greater understanding and appreciation of the "Big Book" of Alcoholics Anonymous. This work provides an outline for the study of that book as well as a reference guide to its contents.

The coverage of the first 164 pages is intended to be exhaustive but the coverage of the story sections only illustrative. That is, entries from the personal stories were selected to amplify and clarify the material contained within the first 164 pages. As such, emphasis was placed upon the stories of the "pioneers of AA" (which includes the story entitled "Our Southern Friend"). All page number references up to and including page 312 are identical for both the second and third editions of the "Big Book". All page number references beyond page 312 refer to the third edition.

I shall be interested to hear from those who are getting results from this reference guide, particularly those who have additions, deletions and changes to offer.

SECTION I

A CONCORDANCE

INTRODUCTION

IDEAS AND CONCEPTS

One of the most frequently used and useful tools for study is a concordance. A concordance is an alphabetical index of words and/or passages in a book or a collection of books by a given author.

The purpose of a concordance is to help locate quickly and accurately an exact word, quotation, phrase or idea. For example, if one wanted to locate the passage: "wreckage of your past" then the keyword in the passsage would be "wreck". Therefore, one would look in the concordance under the W's for the word "wreck". Here would be found:

wreck ....(see also:past)
time to clear away the wreck 123
Wreckage of your past..164

Since the Big Book of Alcoholics Anonymous is a "basic text", this concordance also attempts to organize the words, phrases and passages into coherent and meaningful groups in order to construct ideas and concepts. In the example above, a cross-reference to the keyword "past", enclosed in parenthesis, is provided. Therefore, to find the concept of "past", one would look under the P's for the word "past". within the sub-entries is found a cross-reference to the main entry "thinking". The keyword "thinking" provides yet another "link" in the chain of related ideas and concepts. The relationship among and between ideas and concepts is like a finely woven tapestry.

MAIN ENTRIES AND SUB-ENTRIES

All words, phrases and quotations that appear on the left-hand side of each page are called "main entries". All words, phrases and quotations that are indented to the right and are below a main entry are called "sub-entries". Note that one or more cross-references may appear in both a main entry and in a sub-entry.

For the most part, main entries have been restricted to those words, phrases and quotations which apppear up thru page 164 of the Big Book. The exception to this objective occurs when a word, phrase, or quotation is so engrained in the terminology of the Fellowship that no synonym or near-synonym seems to be a suitable substitute to express the concept being listed and tabulated. Three examples of this exception to the rule are the main entries "blackout", "drunk-a-log" and "surrender". In all three examples, the word neither appears in the Doctor's Opinion nor in the basic text. All three words do, however, appear in the personal stories sections.

WORD FORMS

It is possible to form a vast number of derived forms simply by adding certain prefixes and/or suffixes to a base (or root) word. These affixes establish (1) whether the word is singular or plural, (2) the tense of the word and (3) the usage - part of speech - of the word. For this concordance, the majority of the entries listed are in the noun or verb form, singular mode and present tense. Two exceptions to this word form convention are presented below.

The adjective "great" is used extensively in the Big Book to place emphasis on the central ideas and concepts of the program.

In keeping with this convention, several main entries are listed twice, once in the noun form and again under the general category of "great". For example, the main entry "obsession" has a cross-reference to "great obsession".

The other very notable exception occurs with the root form of the verb "recover". In this case, references to "recovered" and "recovering" are listed separately.

CROSS-REFERENCES

Cross-references enhance the reader's awareness of all other entries pertaining to a given entry. Readers are directed to separate entries by the words "see" and "see also" followed by one or more references. A cross-reference is always a keyword, phrase or quotation. It is used to identify (1) a synonym or an antonym for an entry, (2) the idea or concept in which an entry is categorized or (3) a related keyword, phrase or quotation.

A cross-reference is readily recognized by the pair of parentheses in which it is enclosed. Two or more cross-references are separated by commas within a single set of parenthesis.

ANTONYMS

Antonyms formed by simply adding a prefix such as: dis-, in-, il-, ir-, non-, un-, etc., do not, in most cases, appear in this concordance, nor are words given if they are simple negatives of other words. For example, the word "unselfish" does not appear as a main entry since one may simply look up the positive term. Note however, that "unselfish" does appear as a sub-entry to the main entry "action-attitude". This exception occurs elsewhere in this concordance.

KEYWORDS

The choice of a keyword is not an exact science. A keyword is usually selected on the basis of its uniqueness in a passage or quotation and/or upon common accepted usage.

Keyword concepts and ideas are based upon the recognition of synonyms and equivalent words or expressions. For example, the idea of being "reborn" has the following equivalent expressions: "new life" and "raised from the dead". The word "reborn" can have a symbolic meaning as well as an actual (mystical, religious or spiritual) meaning. By equating: "birth = life", then: "rebirth = rediscovering life."

The word "dead" can also have a figurative meaning as well as an actual meaning. The symbolic analogy of death is graphically portrayed as "the scrap heap" (page ll) and succinctly stated as: "The alcoholic suffers death many times over." (page 457). In other words, the condition of death can be paradoxically stated as a "living death" (page 150). One can now make a very convincing case for the idea that:

"death = bondage"
and "life = freedom"

by recognizing that death and bondage are congruent concepts for the alcoholic as well as are life and freedom. Hence the passage: "engaged upon a life-and-death errand" (page 75) can be understood to mean engaged in a transition from bondage to freedom.

COLLATING SEQUENCE

As a concordance is an alphabetical index, the main entries follow one another in alphabetical order, character-by-character. The ordering rule specifies that a blank preceeds a letter, a letter preceeds a hyphen and a hyphen preceeds a blank. For example:

self
self evident
selfish
selfishness
self-will

is a correct ordering sequence. An exception to the ordering rule occurs for sub-entries. In this case, only the first word of each sub-entry is alphabetized according to the rule given above.

ABBREVIATIONS & CONTRACTIONS

Those main entries which contain abbreviations are alphabetized as if the abbreviations were spelled out. For example, "Dr." is ordered as if it were spelled as "Doctor". Contractions are also ordered as if they are spelled out. For example, the contraction "I'm" is ordered as "I am".

ARTICLES

The indefinite articles "a", "an", and the definite article "the" are, in most cases, dropped from a phrase in this concordance. For example, "a way of life" is listed as "way of life". The exception occurs when a phrase can have a different meaning than the one intended. For example, "a way out" is not listed as "way out".

CAPITALIZTION

By convention, the expression "Twelve Steps" is capitalized. When a particular step is being referenced the number of the step as well as the word "step" is capitalized - for example, the "First Step" or "Step One". When the word "step" is used in a phrase such as "this intimate and confidential step" on page 29, it is not capitalized.

DASH

A dash is frequently used to set off an appositive of a supplementary word or phrase that is added for emphasis or for explanation of an entry. Therefore, the dash and the comments are ignored in the ordering process by treating them as blank characters.

ELLIPSIS

An ellipsis (...) is used to denote the omission of a word or words necessary for complete grammatical construction but understood in the context in which it is used. In this concordance, an ellipsis is used to stress the essence of a phrase. The complete grammatical construction should be easily recognizable from the given segment(s).

NUMBERS

Those main entries which contain an arabic numeral or numerals are alphabetized as if the numeral(s) was spelled out. For example, "Step 12" is ordered as "Step Twelve".

TABULATION

This concordance records the occurrence of a word, phrase or quotation by referencing the page number(s) upon which the item to be included appears. There may be one or more occurrences of an entry on a given page. Exact and explicit tabulation of each occurrence of a given word, phrase or quotation is provided only for selected entries such as "had to", "must" and "simple".

Tabulation by page number rather than by page and line number enables the reader to understand the word, phrase or quotation in its larger context and therefore he or she will be less likely to misinterpet or misuse a reference.

A

a way out .... (see:message)
abandon .... (see:surrender)
abandon - attributes:
  complete 59
  utterly 63
aberrations .... (see:behavior)
abilities .... (see:human resources)
abnormal:
  abnormal drinker 30
  aware of being somehow abnormal 155
  bodily and mentally different 30
  body...as abnormal as his mind xxiv
  reacts differently 22
  these drinkers are abnormal 23
above:
  all else .... (see:First Things First)
  all things .... (see:great obsession)
  everything .... 62, (see also:First Things First)
absolute:
  certainty 25
  necessity 14
absolutely .... xxiv, 17, 24, 39, 40, 58, 120, 132, 155
abstinence .... (see:disease-secondary care)
absurd .... (see:behavior)
abuse .... (see:behavior)
accept .... (see:surrender)
acceptance .... 295, 449, (see also:tolerance)

A

accepting what we have to offer xxv
action - idea of:
    demonstration 14, 19, 49, 78, 98
    Dr. Bob's reasons 181
    faith without works is dead 14, 76, 88, 93, 97
    intentions and actions 83, 450
    seeing is believing 83, 135
action - attitude:
    absence of profit motive xxv
    altruistic xxiv
    give freely 164
    Good Samaritan 97
    happiness...in giving 159,
        (see also:service)
    joy of helping others 164
    self-sacrifice 15, 93
    to be helpful .... (see:service)
    to be of maximum service .... (see:purpose)
    unselfish .... xxv, 93
actor 60-61, 73,
    (see also:play,will)
admit .... (see:surrender)
adopt 11, 114, 130, 143, 153, 163
affairs 14, 19, 60
    (see also:useful/-ness)
affliction .... (see:alcoholism as...)
agree 17, 50, 93
ailment .... (see:alcoholism as...)

alcoholic:
actual 39, 149
of the hopeless variety 44
potential 2, 33-34, 39, 149
real 21, 23, 30, 35, 92, 109
true 44, 109
alcoholic - real or true:
earmarks of a real alcoholic 109
picture of the true (or real) alcoholic 21-22
alcoholism as:
addiction .... xxv, 162
affliction .... xiv, xxv, 92
ailment 135
allergy .... (see:allergy)
condition 32, 42, 113
deficiency 120
disease 64, 187, 191
disorder 58, 114
habit .... xxvi, 20, 91, 140
illness 18, 44, 92, 107, 115, 118, 139, 142
malady 23, 64, 92, 138, 139
terrible curse 180
alcoholism as a spiritual:
condition
- fit spiritual condition 85
- maintenance of 85
deficiency 120
disease 64
malady 64

A

alcoholism attributes ....(see also:insanity-attributes)
    cunning, baffling & powerful 58,
        (see also:baffling, cunning)
    subtle foe 85
alibis .... (see:fallacious reasoning)
allergy .... (see:alcoholism as...)
    may be the manifestation of xxviii
    is a manifestation of xxvi
    we have an allergy xxiv
alone:
    alone in his room 56
    came to live almost alone 105
    God alone can judge 69
    inability to leave it alone 34
    jittery and alone 163
    leave him alone 113
    leave such a person alone 96
    leaving liquor alone for one year 34
    living too much alone 119,
        (see also:isolation)
    no more "aloneness" 312
    see your man alone 91
    take (it /your liquor) or leave it alone 20, 139
    use of this book alone 144
alpha and the omega .... (see:ego)
alternatives .... (see:disease-course)
altruistic .... (see:action-attitude)

A

always & never:
- always .... xxviii, 31, 36, 44, 60, 69, 74, 81, 84, 101, 105, 124, 125, 127, 151, 161
- never .... xxvi, xxviii, 13, 25, 26, 27, 30, 31, 50, 51, 57, 68, 77, 78, 87, 89, 90, 95, 97, 105, 111, 117, 120, 123, 127, 133, 151, 158

Amen 76
amends .... (see:housecleaning)
analysis .... (see:thinking)
anger 64
- dubious luxury 66
- first principle of success .... 111, (see also:success)
- free of 66, 67
- plague 98
- poison 66
- why we were angry .... 64, (see also:threats to self)

anonymous .... xiii, 19
answer .... xxix, 7, 18, 56, 86, 110, 115, 138, 164, (see also:message)
answer - to questions .... (see:questions,riddle)
answer...specifically .... 20, (see also:precisely...,purpose)
antagonism 48
antipathy 12

A

anti-religious 45,
(see also:religion/religious)
anti-social .... (see:isolation)
anxious:
that we talk to the right person 74
that you understand 121
to adopt any workable method 163
to proceed at once 95,
(see also:urgency)
to see us 40
urge them not to be over-anxious 91
any lengths/extreme 58, 76, 79, 90, 198
loss of his job 146
personal consequences 79
risks 80
arch:
cornerstone 47, 56
foundation 75
foundation stone 97
keystone 62
spiritual structure 47
arrested - the alcoholism .... (see:subject matter)
argument .... (see:contention)
arrange 60, 88, 120, 122,
(see also:control)
arrogance .... (see:ego)
asylum 7, 15, 31, 35, 38, 114
at once .... (see:urgency)
at the end of my rope 515,
(see also:bottom)

A

attitude 19, 55, 77, 103, 117, 122
a new pair of glasses 451
analogy of the eyes 12, 280
intollerance & belligerent denial 570
change in 25, 50, 84, 311, 449
new 72, 85, 99, 150
proper 86,
(see also:right)
simple 27,
(see also:simple)
authentication xiii
at meetings - in a general way 58
confession .... xvi, 25, 74, 77
disclose 29, 57, 58, 64, 74, 78, 164
evidence 48
sharing xxii
testimony .... xxiii, 55, 58
with another 73
witness
- step three 63, 446
- step five 74
- step ten 84
authority .... (see:majesty)
avocation .... xiii,
(see also:work)

B

baffling........23, 26, 34, 51, 58, 62, 84, 92, 107, (see also:alcoholism attributes)
banker, nurse & landlord........(see:dependence)
bargaining with God........271-272, 324, 504
barriers........56, 115, 126, (see also:block, handicaps, obstacles)
bed:
    man in/on the bed........157, 188, (see also:App.3)
    take up their beds........19
bedevilments (8 of them)........52, 105-106, (see also:calamities,disaster,promises,troubles)
beer experiment........(see:drinking patterns)
beg (of) you:
    to be fearless and thorough........58
    to lay aside prejudice........49
beginning........19, 63, 71, 118
behavior patterns........22, (see also:conduct,past)
    aberrations........140
    adventures........60
    antics........141
    derelictions........143
    distorted & exaggerated world........108
    distortion of values........129, (see also:excess)
    escapades........91, 123
    exploits........145
    scrapes........140

B

behavior - attributes ..... (see also:experience)
- absurd 21, 37, 87
- appalling 108
- baffling ..... (see:baffling)
- funny 123
- humiliating 123
- incomprehensible 37
- incredible 7, 21, 141
- shameful 123
- shocking 145
- tragic 21, 123
- belittle ..... (see:judgement)

belladonna treatment 7

bender ..... (see:relapse)

better than gold 129

beyond human aid 24, 25, 128,
(see also:human resources)

binge ..... (see:relapse)

blackout 353, 375
- blacked/blacking out 244, 306, 404
- "Blanks" 226
- I know little of where I went 41
- I remember nothing 179
- vaguely remembers 73

blame ..... (see:past,responsibility)

blessing 100, 116, 119, 180, 574

blind:
- blind 13, 107
- could not, or would not, see 16,
(see also:willingness)
- does not see 34, 107, 109, 110

B

block .... (see also:barriers,handicaps,obstacles)

  self-will has blocked you 71

  had been blocking us 64

bondage .... (see also:release)

  bondage of hatred 53

  bondage of self 63

  freedom from bondage .... (see:first promise)

  prayer - freedom from self 87

bottom 315,

(see also:at the end...deflation, lost,turning point)

  badly mangled 43

  broke & homeless 96

  hard knocks 98

  high & low 152

  homeless, jobless, penniless, & rudderless 278

  scrap heap 11, 296

  skid row 319, 379

  skid row of success 345

  start from the bottom and work up 284

bout .... (see:relapse)

break - give me 197-198

Broad Highway 55, 75

business:

  if he means .... (see:Step 12)

  I'm ready to do business 159

bust .... (see:relapse)

But for the grace of God 25,

(see also:mottoes)

C

calamity 6, 46, 55, 56, 68, 116,
(see also:bedevilments,disaster)
camaraderie 17,
(see also:fellowship)
came to believe 59,
(see also:App.3)
cannot or will not .... (see:willingness)
capitalize .... (see:growth)
career - drinking career 21, 123
carry the message .... (see:message,Step 12)
cast:
cast its ashes about 124
cast out 72,
(see also:inventory)
cast to one side 27
causes & conditions .... xxvi, 64, 544
chance .... (see:Step 12-purpose)
change .... (see also:spiritual)
changed attitude 144
emotional rearrangement 27
of heart 55, 143
outlook on life 84
personality change 569
profound:
- alteration 569
- change in personality 572
psychic xxvii
their habits on your account 102
character .... (see:human resources)
charity .... (see:dependence)

C

child:
- childhood.......45
- childishness.......130
- childish faith.......52
- sick or wayward child.......130

choice:
- God either is, or He isn't.......53, (see also:either/or)
- lack of power.......45, (see also:dilemma)
- last promise.......11, 25, 70, 84
- like men who have lost their legs.......30
- now you have a choice.......463
- power of choice/to choose.......24, 34, 59, 334

Christ, Jesus.......11, 236, 536

clean house.......(see:housecleaning)

clear-cut.......29, (see also:directions,precisely)

common:
- common manifestations - of self.......64, (see also:threats to self)
- common sense.......13, 22, 77, 107, (see also:human resources)
- common to most denominations.......94
- has much in common with these people.......131

common ground.......122
- love.......(see:love)
- tolerance.......(see:tolerance)
- understanding.......(see:understanding)

common: - alcoholics have much in common 95
journey 153, 312,
(see also:path)
lot 455,
(see also:bedevilments)
peril 17, 312
solution 17, 50, 312
suffering 573
symptom xxviii
concede .... (see:surrender)
conceit .... (see:ego)
conception of God .... (see:God-idea of)
condemn .... (see:judgement)
condition:
alcoholic .... (see:alcoholism as...)
hopeless 42
relieved 42
spiritual .... (see:alcoholism as a spiritual...)
condition - trust in God to clean house 98,
(see also:requirements)
conduct 38, 70,
(see also:behavior,lesson)
confession .... (see:authentication)
conscious .... (see also:God consciousness)
companionship 56
contact 59, 87
consequences 24, 37, 41, 79,
(see also:any length,thinking)
considered .... (see:thinking)
contempt .... (see:judgement)

C

contention 19, 118,
(see also:anger,judgement)
argument 19, 67, 98, 102, 108, 127
contradict 94
contribute ..... (see:purpose)
contrition 126
control 5, 52, 92, 117, 139, 155,
(see also:arrange,great obsession,
ppt, truth)
after the first drink 21, 32, 44
controlled drinking 31-32
couldn't control our emotional natures 52,
(see also:bedevilments)
lack of; lost; no;
could not; inability ..... xxiv, 23-24, 26
30, 31, 109,
(see also:lack of)
mental control ..... xxvii, xxviii
methods of control 31
miracle of control 151
no real alcoholic ever recovers control 30,
(see also:alcoholic)
convictions:
agnostic 29
announce our convictions 77
convictions have not worked 93
last flicker of conviction 42
moral & philosophical 62,
(see also:human resources)

no matter what your convictions are 93
out of his hope, there burst conviction 189
religious convictions 27
spiritual convictions 130
our convictions 77
Presence of God 51, 56, 162
religious 27, 93
spiritual 77, 93, 130
convince - how not to 96,
(see also:pass it on-how not to)
force yourself upon him 90
lecture/tell him 18, 91, 111, 121
lecture, moralize & condemn 142
not crowd 113
persuade him 90
pressure 91, 94
pushed or prodded 95
tell him what he must do 111, 144
threats, loss & suffering 36, 138
urging him to follow our program 113
convinced .... (see also:disease-diagnosis,self)
any life run on self-will 60
beyond the shadow of a doubt 135
cannot recover by himself 92, 96, 186
cannot postpone or evade 53,
(see also:postpone,urgency)
it is an illness 30

C

convinced (cont'd)
it is life-and-death 75, 540,
(see also:death,errand)
no reservations 33, 187
of the need xvi
self...had defeated us 64
cornerstone .... (see:arch)
count your blessings 119, 355,
(see also:blessing)
craving .... (see also:temptation)
after the first drink .... (see also:insanity)
for alcohol .... xxvi, xxvii, 134, 143
for fellowship 15-16, 164,
(see also:fellowship,needs)
Creator .... (see:God-titles of)
creditors 96,
(see also:fear)
crisis 53,
(see also:blame)
criticize .... (see:judgement)
crux of the problem 35,
(see also:disease-primary care)
cunning 30, 61,
(see also:alcoholism-attributes,denial)
cunning, baffling & powerful 58
cure(d) .... (see:subject matter)
curse .... (see:alcoholism as...)
cycle .... (see:merry-go-round)

D

daily/day:
- daily renewal 237
- daily reprieve 85
- daily work xxvi
- day by day 99, 100
- every day 85, 97
- twenty four hours 16, 86, 188

death 21, 24, 30, 33, 44, 107, 154,
(see also:fatal,perish)
- gates of death xxv
- gates of insanity or death 30
- life and death errand 75
- living death 150, 457
- raised from the dead 11,
(see also:reborn)
- to drink is to die 15, 66, 457,
(see also:convinced)

debacle 22
debauch 8, 104
decide/decision .... (see:diseasse-diagnosis)
decision - to quit drinking .... xxviii, 59, 71,
(see also:methods of control)
- oaths 31, 105
- promises 5
- resolves/resolutions .... xxviii, 34, 107

deep:
- deep down 55
- from within 95
- inner resource 570

D

deep (cont'd):
innermost selves (gut-level) 30
power of God goes deep! 114
defeated - by self .... (see:victory&defeat)
defects of character 50, 59, 72, 99, 100, 118,
(see also:flaws,off/on,shortcomings)
defense 24, 43
defense shield/wall 18, 107, 226,
(see also:isolation)
deficiency 13, 110, 120, 131,
(see also:bottom,ego)
deflation 122,
(see also:ego)
delirium tremens 13, 110
delusion .... (see:self-deception)
demonstration .... (see:action-idea of)
denial .... (see also:cunning,self-deception)
belligerent denial 570
prove themselves exceptions 31
dependence .... (see also:faith in...)
banker, nurse & landlord 95
charity 98, 161
(see also:thinking)
money, connections or shelter 96
service plane 98,
(see also:plane)
derelictions .... (see:behavior)
derided .... (see:judgement)
design for living 15, 28, 81, 340,
(see also:way of life)

desire/want to .... 32, 33, 34, 109, 141, 148, (see also:willingness)
desire to drink .... (see:temptation)
despair .... xxvii, 8, 15, 50, 110, 151, 155, (see also:hopeless)
desperation .... xvii, xxix, 29, 35, 96, (see also:hopeless)
    desperately wants to stop 17, 28, 161
    I'll do anything .... 158, 187, (see also:App.2,willingness)
    shipwreck 17, 28, 161
destitution .... (see:bottom)
determination .... (see:human resources)
devil - expressions 125, 149, 159
Devil 11
diagnosis .... (see:disease-diagnosis)
dictates .... 100, (see also:direction)
difficulties 15, 63, 94
dilemma .... (see also:great obsession)
    defined .... xvi, 28, 45, 152, 380
    solution to 522
direction:
    care and direction .... (see:Step 3)
    carefully followed directions 85
    direction and strength 13, 79
    direction from Him 85
    mother...gave directions 131
    much direction and advice 121
    new sense of power and direction 46

D

directions .... (see:Twelve Steps)
director .... (see:actor,God-titles of)
disaster 17, 27, 44, 152,
(see also:bedevilments,calamity)
disclose .... (see:authentication)
discover .... xix, 46, 63, 64, 72, 90,
99, 106, 116, 159, 164
disease .... (see also:alcoholism as...,App.1)
  not a moral issue/stigma! 227, 448
  not just a "weakness" 371
  two fold nature 380
  spiritual .... (see:alcoholism as a spiritual)
disease - diagnosis .... (see also:convinced)
  decide/decision - for himself 92, 95, 113, 144
  doctor is willing/will tell him 92, 144
  had made his own diagnosis xxix
  you can quickly diagnose yourself 31
disease - chronic .... xxv, 27,
(see also:relapse,repeat)
  irreversible .... xxv, 38
  relapse .... xx, 26, 35, 120, 125, 157,
(see also:relapse)
  slip 100, 139, 181, 271,
294, 320, 343, 416
  stumble 8, 70, 113, 147, 160
  trouble 271
disease - course or progression:
  alternatives 7, 24, 25, 44
  progressive illness 30, 33

disease - mortality & morbidity:
percentage of successes .... xx, 144, 163, (see also:success)
prevalent 149
never touch more than a fair fraction .... xxi, (see also:monopoly)
disease - prognosis:
doomed .... (see:hopeless)
hopeless .... (see:hopeless)
prophesy 41
recovery .... (see:message,Step 12-purpose)
disease - primary care .... (see also:prevalence)
crux of the problem 35
main idea 218
main problem .... (see:problem)
mental states, etc .... (see:mental)
repeats time after time 35
disease - secondary care .... (see also:sobriety is enough)
abstinence .... xiv, xxviii, 30, 409
cessation 122
dry 32, 41, 151, 179, 245
elimination 19
relief xxviii
teetotaler 139
disease - tertiary care:
convalescence 127, 129
development 118
readjustment 122, 146
reconstruction 83
rehabilitation .... xxiii, xxvi, xxix, 7, 148

D

distinction .... (see:thinking)
distrust/skepticism 83, 141
distorted & exaggerated world 108,
(see also:behavior)
distortion of values 129,
(see also:behavior,excess)
Dr. Jekyl & Mr. Hyde 21, 339
domestic troubles .... (see:past)
doomed .... (see:hopeless)
drinking patterns:
how long or how much 33
whisky & milk story 36
what age 33
what kind/switching 31, 177, 203
drowning men 28,
(see also:desperation)
drunk-a-log 396
account of the struggles 92,
(see also:struggles)
cited cases out of their own experience 42
for an hour...about their drinking 157
long drawn out talks 273
recount and almost relive 132
turn the talk to some phase of drinking 91
what we used to be like 58
willing to bring former mistakes 124
dry .... (see:disease-secondary care)

E

earmarks........ 109,
(see also:traits)
easy:
easier, softer way........ 135
Easy Does It........ 135,
(see also:mottoes)
life was not easy........ 156
simple, but not easy........ 14,
(see also:simple)
take it easy........ 86
that was not easy........ 42
turned to easier methods........ 72
we do not tire so easily........ 88
educational variety........ 569,
(see also:spiritual...)
effort........(see:work)
ego........(see also:deflation,faith in...,superiority)
alpha and the omega........ 49
arrogance
- contempt........ 412
- Philistine........ 537
- "special" person........ 536
- I'd prove...I was important........ 2
cockiness/cocky........85, 303
pride........7-8, 12, 25, 75
taking credit for sobriety........ 203,
(see also:grace...)
vanity........ 116,
(see also:human resources)

E

ego-centric 61
ego - examples 348, 445, 534-535
either/or 53, 120, 142
elements 57,
(see also:essentials,fundamentals)
emotional appeal - frothy xxvii
emotional swings 560,
(see also:roller coaster)
Employer .... (see:God-titles of)
enemies:
greatest enemies - 5 of them 145
harder to go to an enemy 77
our former enemies 78
toward all men, even our enemies 70
energy 88
envy - from normal people .... (see:fellowship,jealousy)
errand 75, 102,
(see also:convinced,death)
escape .... xxviii, 66, 94, 152,
(see also:disaster,reasons for drinking)
escapades .... (see:behavior)
essentials - HOW 13-14, 47-48, 550, 570,
(see also:elements,fundamentals)
evade 5, 53
evidence .... (see:authentication)
evil 7,
(see also:fear)
exact:
nature of our defects 2
nature of our wrongs 9

exception 31, 39,
(see also:it doesn't fully apply)
excess 5, 119, 125-126, 128, 146, 149, 156,
(see also:behavior)
excuses/"reasons" .... (see also:fallacious reasoning)
excuse to postpone 5,
(see also:postpone,urgency)
misunderstood 11
no excuse 3, 40, 107
silly or trivial excuse 7, 42, 107, 120
expect 8, 74, 95, 99, 101,
18, 120, 126, 149
expectations 52
experience .... (see also:past,practical,
spiritual,theory)
drinking 22-23, 33, 39, 42, 91, 92, 155, 157
experience .... xiii, 70, 84, 101, 103, 116,
121, 134, 137
working the program 19, 29, 44, 50, 72, 85, 89
experience - attributes .... (see also:past-attributes)
bitter 39
painful 121
practical 89
experience, strength & hope xxii
ex- .... (see also:subject matter-cured)
alkie 311
drunks .... (see:Sect.II-earlier editions)
problem drinkers .... xxiv, 18, 20, 151,
(see also:problem-alcohol)

F

face:

his problems squarely 156

life successfully 63

the fact 44

the proposition 53,

(see also:either/or)

fact 24, 51, 55, 64, 70, 119

central fact 25

great fact 25

Great Fact 164

tremendous fact 17

fair-weather 3, 122, 296,

(see also:friends)

faith - idea of .... (see also:authentication)

acceptance without proof 48

childish faith 52

self-evident .... xii, 9,

(see also:it works)

faith - inability to accept 47,

(see also:handicaps)

faith alone is insufficient 93

faith in other things .... (see also:ego)

alcohol 499

human resources 53,

(see also:human resources)

people, places & things 54, 99,

(see also:dependence)

worship of other things 55

faith without works is dead .... (see also:action-idea of)

F

fallacious reasoning..23,
(see also:ego,insanity)
alibis..23,
(see also:rationalization)
excuses..(see:excuses)
justification..37
fatal..66, 142,
(see also:death,perish)
Father..(see:God-titles of)
fault:
admit(ting)...faults..77, 81, 164
family be at fault..98
fault-find..(see:contention)
his faults are not discussed..78
not entirely our fault..67
they are not at fault..58
through no fault of her own..131
where were we at fault..69
fault-find..(see:judgement)
fear..52, 62, 67-68, 73, 75, 78, 84, 104,
115-116, 120, 154,
(see also:bedevilments,evil,
enemies,growth,self)
feelings:
communication of..451
harboring..(see:resentment)
fellowship..xxiii, 45, 90, 153
fellowship..(see also:camaraderie,frequent)
benefits of..152, 312
craving for..(see:craving)

F

fellowship (cont'd):
envy - from normal people 334,
(see also:normal people)
meetings 159, 246, 291
offer him friendship & fellowship 95,
(see also:relationship)
sociability & problems 160-161
social distinctions 17, 152, 161,
(see also:shipwreck)
substitute 152
versus the program 144, 163, 164, 340, 381
fellowship - early AA:
get togethers 159, 245
indoctrination & instruction 185, 291
informal meetings 162
inventories - taking each others 245
old-time A.A 272
sponsorship 292
twos and threes and fives .... xv, 162
Fellowship .... xiii, xv, xix, xxii,
94, 96, 159, 161, 164
Fellowship of the Spirit 164
fighting & defiance 84, 103, 226
financial recovery 127,
(see also:material success)
first:
aid 132
drink 23, 24, 37, 40, 41, 43, 157,
(see also:insanity)

first (cont'd):
- promise ....83, 133, 208, (see also:bondage)
- requirement .... 60, (see also:requirements)
- step in recovery .... 30, (see also:concede)

First Things First ....(see also:mottoes)
- material success 127, 130, 507
- other habits.... 135, 190
- recovery above all else....143, 153, 452, (see also:recovery,success)
- sobriety above all else.... 293, 409
- wish them above all else 153

fix....6, 40, 157

fixed ideas....(see:prejudice)

flaws in our make-up .... 64, (see also:defects...,off/on,shortcomings)

fool of the first magnitude.... 137

forces .... (see also:human resources)
- guiding forces 27
- gathering all his forces 32

forgiveness .... (see:prayer-ask for)

foundation....(see also:arch)
- cement put into the foundation 75
- of complete willingness 12

foundation stone....(see:arch)

Four Horsemen 151

F

fourth dimension........8, 25,
(see also:God-consciousness)
free man........26, 28, 75, 158,
(see also:bondage)
freedom:
a new freedom and a new happiness........83
arch through which we passed to freedom........62
freedom from bondage........544,
(see also:first promise)
freedom from fear and despair........430
highroad to a new freedom........xxi
real freedom........553
stepped over the threshold...into freedom........160
freely given........(see:grace...)
frequent........(see also:fellowship)
frequent contact........89
one night a week........159
we meet frequently........15
friend........(see:relationship with newcomers)
friends:
fair-weather........3, 296, 358
high-stepping........120
so-called........293
Friend........(see:God-titles of)
frothy emotional appeal........xxvi
fundamentals........120,
(see also:elements,essentials)

game .... (see also:great obsession)
drinking game 91
try the old game again 152
get-togethers .... (see:fellowship-early AA)
gifts 21,
(see also:grace...)
girl who understands 81, 106, 124
give 98, 158, 159, 164
giving versus getting .... (see:purpose,service)
God - idea of .... (see also:ideas)
as/you understand him 13, 46, 59, 63, 164
conception of God 12, 46-47, 93
idea of 55, 248, 569,
(see also:ideas)
Jim B's contribution 248
personal 10, 12, 236,
(see also:God-relationship)
possible - with God 55, 62
God - idea of power .... (see also:possible,power)
All Powerful 49, 161
has all knowledge and power 85
has all power 59
Infinite Power and Love 56
power of God 13, 52, 114, 130
power of/which is God 46, 162
God - idea of infinite:
impossible...to fully define or comprehend 46
infinite God...finite selves 68
infinite Power and Love 56

G

God - discovery of .... (see also:deep,discover)
discovered...another's conception of God 46
discovery of God 116
had found God...had found himself 158
had to find a power 45,
(see also:had to)
God - relationship .... (see also:dependence,God's hands)
assistance 98
dependence 52, 68, 100
relationship 13, 29, 72, 100, 164
reliance 68, 164
trust 68, 98,
(see also:condition)
with Him is right 164
God - relationship with:
we don't...shying away
from the subject of God 77
we never apologize to anyone 68
we stand on our feet; we
don't crawl before anyone 83
God - titles of .... (see also:App.7,power)
Creative Intelligence 12, 46, 49
Creator 13, 25, 28, 56, 68, 72, 75,
76, 80, 83, 158, 161
Director 62,
(see alsos:actor)
Employer 63
Father 14, 39, 62, 104, 115,
123, 126, 127, 131

God - titles of (cont'd)
Father of Light 14
Friend........ 13
Great Physician........ 351,
(see also:miracles)
Great Reality........ 55, 16 l
(see also:God-idea of)
Maker........ 57, 63
Power 46, 47, 50, 56
Principal........ 62
Spirit........ 66, 84, 85
Spirit of Nature........ 12
Spirit of the Universe........ 10, 46, 52, 75
Supreme Being........ 46
God consciousness........ 13, 51, 85, 270, 569, 570,
(see also:conscious)
fourth dimension 8, 25
inspiration 85, 86, 87,
(see also:plane)
intuitive........ 86
sixth sense........ 85
God did for us what we
could not do for ourselves .... (see:choice-last promise)
God's hands........ 100, 120, 124,
(see also:let go)
good news........ (see:message)
Good Samaritan .... (see:action-attitude)
good will .... (see:love)
gossip .... (see:sensitiveness)

G

grace gift & gratitude..........(see also:pass it on, obligation/duty)
grace..........25, 367, 399, (see also:But for...)
gift
- freely given..........14, 19
- give freely..........164
gift
- of sobriety..........85, (see also:neutrality)
- power to help others..........132
gratitude..........(see also:resentment,thankful)
- for God..........11
- for sobriety..........43, 100, 128
- for the program..........192, 260, 334
- for the 12th Step..........94
Great Fact..........(see:fact)
great hope..........xxi
great news..........(see:message)
great obsession..........30, (see also:control,dilemma,game, ideas,self-deception)
clings to the notion..........110
hoping against hope..........44
how he can drink moderately..........109
lurking notion..........33
miracle of control..........151
obsession..........23, 151
recapture the great moments..........9, 151

great obsession (cont'd):
victim to a belief 32
wished above all things
to regain self-control 26
great persuader 48
Great Physician .... (see:God-titles of)
Great Reality .... (see:God-titles of,Presence of God)
greatest posession .... (see:past)
growth 117
capitalize 117, 133
growing pains 124
lifetime process 12, 83, 84, 100, 123, 249,
(see also:time)
lose our fear 78
outgrow
- fear 68
- sensitiveness 125
perfection 60
progress
- fails somewhat in practicing 130
- progress 60, 100
- tried to carry this message 60,
(see also:message)
spiritual growth 47, 66
grudge 65,
(see also:rancor,resentment)

H

habit 102, 118, 148,
(see also:alcoholism as...)
had better 102, 120, 128,
(see also:had to,has to,have to,App. 4)
had to .... (see also:has to,have to,must)
ask ourselves 52
be free of anger 66
face the fact 44
fearlessly face 53
find a power 45
fully concede 30
give to others 158
have God's help 62
place recovery above everything 143
place the outcome in God's hands 80,
(see also:God's hands)
quit playing God 62
stop doubting 52
unify...or pass off the scene xix
unify our fellowship xix
hair of the dog 333,
(see also:Sect.II-earlier editions)
half measures .... (see also:let go,reservations)
half measures 59, 516
middle of the road solution 25
handicaps (4 of them) 47-48, 71, 125,
(see also:barriers,block,obstacles)
handicapped .... xiii, 89
(see also:Step 12-purpose)

H

harbor(ing)....................66, 149,
(see also:resentment)
happy, joyous & free....................133,
(see also:first promise,joy)
harmonious/harmony....................17, 61
has to....................30, 95, 135,
(see also:had to,have to,must)
have to....................79, 81, 83, 103,
(see also:had to,has to,must)
healing....................(see:health,miracle)
herd instinct....................571,
(see also:fellowship)
heaven....................25,
(see also:hereafter,Utopia)
help - outside help....................186
help:
- asked God to help....................67, 80
- divine help....................43
- God's help....................62
- spiritual help....................25, 27
- without help it is too much for us....................59

help:
- given the power to help others....................132,
(see also:grace...)
- must help other alcoholics....................159
- to see them help others....................89
- to someone we can help....................84
- try to help....................90, 94, 96
- you can help when no one else can....................89
- you will do anything to help....................95

H

help:

hope these suggestions will help 148

I don't see how you can...help 148

most people...will be glad to help 116

responsibility for...his help 137

the firm wants to help you 147

we needed this help 116

you want to help him 141

your attempt to understand and help 141

helpful .... (see:service)

hereafter .... 63, (see also:heaven,Utopia)

health 133

hell 4, 6, 27, 56, 81

Higher Power .... (see:power)

high & low .... (see:bottom)

honest .... xxvii, 13, 26, 28, 32, 44, 47, 55, 57, 58, 63, 64, 65, 67,70, 73, 83, 117, 140, (see also:essentials)

entirely 73, 482

honest desire to stop drinking .... xiv, (see also:requirements)

rigorous 58, 145

hope 43, 44, 45, 66, 73, 144

Alcoholics Anonymous .... xv, 103, 153, 162

the book .... xiii, xxi, 108, 163

you are convinced .... 71, (see also:convinced)

H

hopeless .... (see also:human resources)
doomed .... xxvii, xxviii, 44, 92
hopeless 10, 14, 17, 26, 43, 44, 92
hopeless variety - of alcoholic 44
no hope xxix
100% hopeless 43
hopeless state of mind & body .... xiii, 20
housecleaning 63, 73, 94,
(see also:past)
admit...our wrongs 59
amends
- definition 77
- making 83, 381
- wrongs...make right 13, 80, 83
amends - willing to make 69
- take the bit in our teeth 77
- take the bull by the horns 156
clean house 83, 98
house is in order 164
rectify 124
repair 127
reparation 79, 98
restitution xvi
straighten out the past .... (see:past)
trust in God & clean house 98
wrong-doing 66, 80
HOW .... (see:essentials)
how important is it? 452
how we (have) recovered .... xiii, 29

H

human resources 45, 50,
(see also:forces,reliance upon...,self-sufficiency)
abilities 8
character 34
common sense .... (see:impulsive)
determination 40
intelligence/intelligent 26, 38, 227
judgement 40
knowledge 38, 39
money 33
morality & ethics 44, 62
reason 54
will power 24, 33, 34, 62, 155
humility 13, 63, 68, 72-73, 88
our opinion may, of course, mean little xxiv
we cannot answer the riddle 22,
(see also:riddle,why me?)
we know only a little 164

I

I'm sorry....83
I'll do anything....(see:App.2,desperation)
ideals....xxvi, 19, 69, 70,
(see also:prayer-ask for)
ideas....xxiii, 27, 111, 116, 123
absurd....87,
(see also:absurd)
basic....xvii
control & enjoy his drinking....30,
(see also:great obsession)
fixed ideas....(see:prejudice)
foolish idea....37,
(see also:great obsession)
fundamental idea....55,
God idea....45, 52,
(see also:God-idea of)
main idea....218,
(see also:disease-primary care)
old ideas....52, 58,
(see also:life-old life)
our ideas....52
religious idea....9,
(see also:simple)
self-sufficiency....52,
(see also:human resources)
threadbare idea....24,
(see also:great obsession)
three pertinent ideas....60,
illness....(see:alcoholism as...)

I

illusion .... (see:self-deception)
immediate(ly) .... (see:urgency)
immunity .... (see:disease-immunity)
imperative .... xxiv, 14, 143,
(see also:had to,have to,must)
impossible 11, 23, 25, 34, 46, 48, 50, 101,
(see also:possible)
impotence 134,
(see also:sex)
impulsive & undisciplined .... (see:thinking)
impunity .... (see:normal folks)
in A.A. vs on A.A. 250
incompatible 108, 130
inconsistancy:
made worse by...his sprees 73,
(see also:actor)
mental inconsistancies 92
to all appearences 39
to the outer world 73
indecision 86-88,
(see also:prayer-ask for)
indispensable 76, 570,
(see also:essentials)
infinite .... (see:God-idea of)
insanity 38, 551,
(see also:disease-primary care,thinking)
judgement - lack of 107
lack of perspective 5
lack of proportion 37

insanity (cont'd):
main problem 23,
(see also:problem)
mental blank spots 42
mental condition 92
mental phenomenon 37
mental states 35, 157
mental twist 92
of the first drink 37, 92, 154,
(see also:merry-go-round)
insanity - attributes .... (see also:alcoholism attributes)
insidious 8, 154
subtle 40
insecurity:
economic insecurity 84
financial insecurity 18
never financial security 105
inspiration .... (see:God-consscious,prayer)
instantly .... (see:urgency)
instruct .... (see:pass it on-how not to)
insurance policy 181
insure:
his sobriety 129
immunity 89,
(see also:App.1)
intelligence .... (see:human resources)
intentions .... (see:action-idea of)
intervention 137
intimacy 134, 151

I

inventory 59, 64-71, 72, 76
inventory - on paper 64, 69
in black & white 67
list 13, 59, 65, 66, 67, 76
listed 67, 70
written 70, 75
irrational 140,
(see also:behavior)
isolation 131,
(see also:fellowship)
anti-social 21, 151, 549, 551,
(see also:life,society)
communication - lack of 81, 126
loneliness 89, 151, 152
withdraw 102, 151
it doesn't fully apply 38, 94,
(see also:denial,exception)
it works 9, 25, 28, 88, 144,
(see also:design for living,self-evident)
it works if we...work at it 86, 552,
(see also:service,work)

J

jail........78-79, 107
jay-walking story........37-38
jealous(y)........(see also:envy)
  arousing resentment or jealousy........100
  feeling of jealousy may arise........131
  greatest enemies (5 of them)........145
  justified by...jealousy........37
  needlessly vent...jealousy........82
  most terrible human emotion........82
  of a God........128
  of the attention he bestows........119
  petty rivalries and jealousies........161
  unjustifiably arouse jealousy........69
job........102,
(see also:purpose-of individual)
job - getting and staying sober........95
job or no job........98,
(see also:recovery)
John Barleycorn........254, 343, 498
join:
  in brotherly & harmonious action........17
  in his efforts........119
  us........xxi, 55, 164
joy........(see also:happy,joyous&free)
  at our release........128
  in escape from disaster........17
  in our existence........132
  of helping others........164
  of living........15

J

judge:
- God alone can judge 69
- let God be the final judge 70

judgement:
- belittle 133
- condemn 50, 108, 142
- contempt prior to investigation 570
- criticize 13, 77, 89, 111, 117, 118, 125, 126, 127, 129
- derided 131
- fault-find 98
- ridicule 125

judgement ..... 26, 40, 107, 135, (see also:human resources)
- of ideas ..... (see:prejudice)
- of others ..... (see:judgement,resentment)
- of self ..... (see:remorse,self-pity, yesterday...)

justification ..... (see:fallacious reasoning)

K

key:
- to life & happiness 124
- to the future 66

keystone .... (see:arch)
kindness .... (see:love)
knowledge .... (see:human resources)

L

lack of:
- control 21, 109
- judgement .... (see:insanity)
- perspective .... (see:insanity)
- proportion .... (see:insanity)

last promise 25, 70-71, 84
laughter & play 16, 91, 132, 146, 160
learn .... (see also:lesson)
- find these things out for myself 536
- learn these things the hard way 121

leaving aside the drink question .... 51, (see also:bedevilments)
lectures .... (see:convince-how not to)
legitimate reason 101
lesson .... (see also:learn)
- once an alcoholic, always an alcoholic .... 33, (see also:disease-chronic)
- learned our lesson .... 70, (see also:behavior,conduct)

let go .... 58, (see also:abandon,ideas-old,our)
let's look at the record 50
levity .... (see:laughter&play)
life .... (see also:society)
- life-and-death errand .... (see:convinced,errand)
- new life .... (see:reborn)
- old life .... 43, 120, (see also:ideas-old ideas)
- way of life/living .... 8, 16, 84, 99, 117, 124, 153, 160, (see also:design for living)

L

list - increase the list.......18, 31
Live And Let Live.......(see:mottoes)
lifetime process.......(see:growth)
living death.......(see:death)
living sober hints.......100-103
loneliness.......(see:isolation)
Lord's prayer.......(see:prayer-closing)
lost.......(see also:bottom)
  everything worthwhile in life.......xxix
  not lost everything in life.......38,
  (see also:it doesn't fully apply)
  nothing and had found everything.......vii
love.......(see also:fellowship elements)
  goodwill/good will.......16, 19, 70
  kindness.......67, 86
  love.......67, 70, 84, 86, 118, 122, 127
love thy neighbor as thyself.......153, 236
lurking notion.......(see:great obsession)
luxury.......66,
  (see also:anger)

M

main:
- idea 218
- object 45
- problem 23,
  (see also:insanity)
- purpose viii
- thing 93

maintenance:
- and growth of a spiritual experience 66
- of our spiritual condition 85,
  (see also:alcoholism as a spiritual...)

Maker .... (see:God-titles of)
malady .... (see:alcoholism as...)
man on the bed 157, 188,
(see also:App.3)

material:
- material needs 98
- realm of .... (see:realm)
- success .... (see:success)

majesty - authority 56
medical:
- discussion of matters medical 19
- extreme medical importance xxiii
- have a low opinion of alcoholics 73
- neither does AA take any
  particular medical point of view xx

meditation .... (see also:prayer)
- meditation 59, 69, 83, 85, 87, 134, 164
- quiet time 13, 75

M

meetings .... (see:fellowship,frequent)
mend:
his spiritual fences 135
his ways 38
mental:
attitude .... (see:resentment)
blank spots .... (see:insanity)
condition .... (see:insanity)
control .... (see:control)
faculties 86
inconsistencies .... (see:inconsistency)
phenomenon .... (see:insanity)
states .... (see:insanity)
twist .... (see:insanity)
mental:
defectives xxiv
disorders 58
mental attitude .... (see also:life-way of life)
alcoholic mind 41, 42, 101
frame of mind 40
outlook 84, 569
point of view .... xx, 29, 52
tendencies 24, 131
temperament 108
viewpoints 19
merry-go-round 238, 468,
(see also:repeat)

M

message .... xvi, xxvi, 60
  a way out 17, 147, 153, 227
  answer .... xxi, 18, 35, 42, 144, 160
  practical answer 153,
    (see also:practical)
  remedy .... xxiv, 39, 112, 118, 144
  solution .... xxiv, 18, 25, 43, 92, 145, 141
  solution of these bedevilments 52,
    (see also:bedevilments,promises)
message - attributes:
  good news 158
  great news 17, 47
  tidings 11
methods of control 31,
    (see also:drinking patterns)
miracle 11, 85, 128, 161, 280
  age of miracles 153
  miracle of control 151
  miracle of healing 57
  miracle of mental health 133
  miracle of reconciliation 124
  wholesale miracle xv
miraculous 25, 50, 55
misery:
  prey to misery & depression 52,
    (see also:bedevilments)
  stream of misery 163
  trouble and misery 15

M

money 2, 3, 4, 7,
(see also:human resources)
advance the cost of treatment 143
cry for money 98
every means...which money could buy 32-33
if he owes you money
you may wish to make terms 145
lending money/financial assistance 96, 161
most alcoholics owe money 78
never have much money again 123
our pocketbooks .... (see:threats to self)
sharing your money 97
monopoly:
monopoly .... xxi, 95
no desire to convince 28
the last word on this subject 144
virtually no other solution 43,
(see also:message)
we cannot be helpful to all people 67
moral(ity) 45, 59,
(see also:human resources)
moralize .... (see:convince-how not to)
motives .... xxv, 54, 70, 86, 102,
(see also:thinking)
mottoes 135
But for the grace of God 25,
(see also:grace...)
Easy Does It 135

M

mottoes (cont'd)
First Things First 135,
(see also:success)
Live and Let Live 118, 135,
(see also:acceptance,rules,tolerance)
must .... (see:App.4)

N

necessary:
- in the sense we find it 73
- spiritual experience was absolutely 155
- vital spiritual experience 27

need it and want it .... (see:Step 12-purpose)

need:
- needs & wants 553, 560
- of myself .... (see:prayer-ask for)
- of others .... (see:service)

neurotic 122

neutrality 85,
(see also:immunity,spiritually fit, temptation)

never .... (see:always&never)

new 30, 131, 132
- and wonderful ties 152
- arch 62
(see also:arch)
- attitude .... (see:attitude)
- basis 120
- Employer .... (see:God-titles of)
- epoch .... xxiv,
(see also:new light)
- freedom 83
- happiness 83
- ideas 52
- life 28,
(see also:life,reborn)

N

new (cont'd):
light .... xvii,
(see also:new-epoch)
man 134
new-found friend .... (see:God-titles of)
power 50, 63
relationship 13, 72
set of conceptions & motives 27
soil 12
status 135
way of life 99,
(see also:life)
newcomer .... (see also:relationship...)
candidate 94
newcomer 15, 72, 89, 159
prospect 18, 90, 91, 93, 96,
99, 148, 156, 158
protege 92
recruit 102
no matter what:
the subject 118
your own convictions are 93
your present circumstances 100
no opinion on outside issues .... (see:personal affairs)
no respector of persons .... xx, 17, 152, 373, 455,
(see also:social distinctions)
normal:
entirely normal in every respect xxvii
is otherwise a normal individual 113
normal so far as we can see 35

N

normal folks/people:
- other men 31, 32
- other people 30, 31, 81
- impunity xxvii
- observations on drinkers .... 20, 22, 139, 140, (see also:fool...)
- observations on drinking:
  - - go on a drinking spree, and then snap out of it 404
  - - for most normal folks 151
  - - go on a mild bender, get up... and go to business 139

O

obligation/duty 94, 147, 181,
(see also:grace...)
oblivion 6, 19, 151, 184
observations .... (see:normal folks)
obsession - few knew about his drinking 155,
(see also:great obsession)
obstacles 8, 72, 123,
(see also:barriers,handicaps)
obstinacy .... (see:handicaps,perverse streak)
off/on .... (see also:App.5)
off the beam 471
off the track 68
on the right track 100
on the wrong track 98
offended 94,
(see also:contention,Live & Let Live)
one alcoholic talking to another .... xxii, 180,
(see also:identification)
one drink was too much and one
hundred drinks were not enough 380,
(see also:contol,lack of)
once an alcoholic, always an alcoholic 33,
(see also:disease-chronic)
100 members .... tp, xiii, xvii, 42, 246, 248, 257
one year 34,
(see also:time)
open-mindedness .... (see:essentials,tolerance)
opportunity .... (see:Step 12-purpose)
or else 44

O

oral/verbal tradition 291,
(see also:pass it on)
other addictions/habits .... (see:First Things First)
outgrow .... (see:growth)
Oxford Groups .... xvi, 8, 26, 218, 574,
(see also:tenets)

P

paradox 68
  step one 507
  step three 68, 542
  step twelve 542
pass it on 9, 94, 180, 181,
  (see also:oral/verbal...)
pass it on - how not to .... (see also:convince-how not to)
  crusade or reform 95
  evangelist or reformer 89
  fanatics or religious bores 77
  holier than thou 18
  instruct him in religion 93
  nag or killjoy 111
  quack or fanatic 413
  ranting, preaching 9
  reform 111
  religious enthusiast 128
  witchburners 103
pass it on - how to:
  announce our convictions 77
  present their discovery 19, 159
past .... (see also:experience,strength...,
  housecleaning)
  analysis of 83,
  (see also:thinking)
  blame for 67, 127, 133,
  (see also:behavior,responsibility)
  damage done in the past 76

past (cont'd):

  decisions - made in the past .... 62, (see also:thinking)

  domestic troubles .... 125, (see also:girl who...)

  find these things out for myself 536

  forgetfulness of 124

Henry Ford's remark 124

  principal asset - greatest possession 124

  promise

    - second 83

    - our experience can benefit 84

  straighten out .... 70, 77, 94, (see also:straighten)

  wreckage of .... 164, (see also:wreck)

past - attributes .... (see also:behavior-attributes, experience-attributes)

  bitter 39

  dark 124

  musty 11

  painful 121, 124

path .... 58, 72, 100, 116, (see also:common journey)

patience .... 67, 70, (see also:time,tolerance)

  to wives 111, 118

  what we have accomplished 163

P

peace 8, 14, 75, 84,
(see also:serenity)
perfect peace & ease 75
of mind 63,
(see also:serenity)
penality 99,
(see also:relapse)
people, places & things .... (see also:faith in...)
acceptance of 449,
(see also:Live And Let Live)
control of 61-62, 88, 445,
(see also:actor)
dependence upon 66, 98, 472,
(see also:charity)
percentage of successes .... (see:disease-mortality&morbidity)
perfect:
adherence 60
peace & ease 75
perfect & enlarge his spiritual life 14-15
spiritual perfection 60
perfection 16,
(see also:growth)
perish 16, 46,
(see also:death,fatal)
permanent:
effect 64
recovery xvii
release 169,
(see also:quit/stop,release)

P

personal affairs ....(see also:no opinion...,tolerance)
  acquire faith........28
  conception of God........50
  family & the prospect........90
  intimate situations........81-82
  liquor as a social lubricant........110
  religious affiliation........28, 132
  reuniting of family........99-100
  serving liquor........102
  sex situation........69, 81
perspective........(see:consequences,insanity,thinking)
perverse streak........49,
  (see also:obstinacy)
phobias........(see also:fear)
  jumping out of a window........6, 501
  not having enough liquor........22, 175
  not holding a job........548
  not sleeping........175, 440
  others finding out........73, 155, 375
  sense of impending calamity........6,
  (see also:calamity,disaster)
pitiful & incomprehensible demoralization........30
pity........67,
  (see also:charity)
plague:
  argument & fault finding........98
  past misdeeds........124
plane:
  altruistic plane........xxiv
  plane of inspiration........87

P

plane (cont'd):
- service plane .... 98, (see also:dependence)
- spiritual plane .... xxiv, 116
- thought life...on a much higher plane 86

play .... (see also:actor)
- play God .... 62, 506, (see also:God-idea of,purpose)
- play the role He assigns .... 68, (see also:will)

pneumonia 108

point of view .... (see:tolerance)

possible .... (see also:imposible)
- God made these things possible 55
- God makes that possible 62

postpone .... (see also:procrastination)
- excuse to postpone 74-75
- postpone or evade .... 53, (see also:convinced)

potential alcoholic .... (see:alcoholic)

power .... (see also:God-idea of power,-titles of)
- greater than .... xxvi, 10, 12, 45, 46, 47, 48, 50, 55, 59, 93, 163
- Higher Power .... 43, 100, (see also:God-titles of)
- lack of power .... 45, (see also:choice,dilemma)
- sense of power and direction .... 46, (see also:bottom)

power to help others .... (see:grace...)

P

powerless .... (see:choice,Step 1)
practical .... (see also:experience,theory)
    answer .... (see:message)
    approach 160
    experience .... (see:experience-attributes)
    program .... (see:program-attributes)
prayer .... (see also:meditation)
    how to 13, 87
    meetings
        - opening 270
        - closing 270, 291
    resentment you want to be free of 552
    serenity prayer 382
    step three (willingness) 63
    step seven (shortcomings) 76
    step ten (anger) 67
    when to pray 86-87
prayer - don't ask for 13, 87
prayer - ask for .... (see also:right)
    direct our attention/thinking 68, 86
    direction 13, 85,
        (see also:bottom,power)
    forgiveness 86
    freedom from self-will 87
    guidance 70
    inspiration 85, 86,
        (see also:plane)
    mold our ideals 69,
        (see also:ideals)
    outgrow fear 68

P

prayer - ask for (cont'd):
power ... 59
right answer ... 69
right ideal ... 70,
(see also:ideals)
right thought or action ... 87
sanity ... 70
strength ... 76, 85
success ... 219
to be helpful ... 164,
(see also:action-attitude,service)
precepts ... 93
precisely how we have recovered ... xiii,
(see also:answer specifically,clear-cut)
prejudice ... 12, 47, 55, 570,
(see also:handicaps)
biased & unreasonable ... 51
fixed ideas ... 51, 122, 570,
(see also:ideas)
organized religion ... 49
shortcomings ... 11, 50, 127
the world and its people ... 66
Presence of God ... (see:convictions,Great Reality)
pressure ... (see:convince-how, not to)
prevalent ... (see:disease...)
price to be paid ... 14, 108, 155,
(see also:self-getting rid of)
pride ... (see:ego)
principal asset ... (see:past)

principles:

basic principles of the A.A. program....xxii

first principle of success.... 111,
(see also:anger,success)

general principles 79, 94,
(see also:religious)

guiding principle.... 128,
(see also:giving,purpose,service)

new principles 98

principles 60, 130

same principle - not embarrass or harm.... 115

simple principles.... 130,
(see also:simple)

spiritual principles 42, 93, 156,
(see also:Twelve Steps)

stick to your own story.... 125,
(see also:sensitiveness)

problem .... (see also:neutrality,temptation)

alcohol/drinking/liquor....19, 32, 101,
(see also:subject matter)

- disappeared 56-57, 75

- no longer a problem 119

- removed 85, 120

- solved....17, 25, 104

- taken away.... 56

crux of the problem.... 35

main problem.... 23,
(see also:insanity)

P

problem (cont'd):
other problems....29, 40, 52, 55, 87, 90, 160, (see also:bedevilments,leaving aside...)
- domestic problems....98-100
- fear problems....68
- health problems....133
- sex problems....69
responsibility for....(see:responsibility)
spiritual principles/remedy....39, 42
problems - after sobriety....(see also:growth)
manageable or disappear....448
ups & downs....(see:roller coaster)
will not be solved at once....117, (see also:time)
procrastination....197, (see also:postpone)
program....(see also:Twelve Steps)
of action....9, 42
of recovery....xi, 59, 72, 96, 147
program - attributes:
practical....9, (see also:practical)
simple....58, (see also:simple)
spiritual....126, 130
useful....19
progress....(see:growth)
progressive illness....(see:disease-course)
promises - to quit drinking....(see:decision-to quit...)

promises:
after the 3rd step - all sorts of remarkable 63
after the 5th step - Once we have taken 75
before we are halfway through 83-84,
(see also:App.6,bedevilments)
great events will come to pass 164
remarkable things 63, 100
promptly .... (see:urgency)
proof .... (see:faith-idea of)
proper .... (see also:right)
attitude .... (see:attitude)
time and place 102
use of the will .... (see:will)
prophesy .... (see:disease-course)
proportionality 68, 452, 551
proposition .... (see:either/or)
prospect .... (see:newcomer)
protestations 62
purpose:
great cause to live for 119
great sense of purpose 130
to play the role He assigns 68,
(see also:play God)
purpose .... (see also:subject matter)
of book .... xiii, 20, 45, 143-144
of individual 77, 102, 551,
(see also:prayer-Step 7)
of twelfth step .... (see:Step 12-purpose)

P

purpose - indirect references ....(see also:service)

think of what you can bring to it 102

think of what you can put into life 120

what you can do each day 164,

(see also:daily/day)

what we could do/contribute....................63, 86

purpose - indirect ref. to 12th Step -

showing others who suffer....................124-125

Q

questions - that this book will answer....22, 107-108, (see also:riddle)
quickly....(see:urgency)
quiet - pause after step five....75, (see also:urgency)
quiet time....(see:meditation)
quit/stop....(see also:permanent)
  for good....90, 112, 181
  forever....116, 142
  never going to want another drink....206-207
  stop altogether....34
  stop while there is yet time....32-33
  wants to stop but cannot....25, 110
quit upon a nonspiritual basis....34, (see also:choice)

R

rancor 111, 134,
(see also:grudge,resentment)
rationalization 551,
(see also:fallacious reasoning)
re -
reborn 63
re-create their lives xxvi
rediscover life 153
real alcoholic .... (see:alcoholic)
real function - of AA 216
Reality, Great .... (see:God-titles of)
realm:
mad realm 151
of the material 51
of the Spirit 46, 51,
(see also:Spirit)
reason .... (see:human resources)
reasons for drinking:
craving .... xxviii,
(see also:control)
effect .... xxvi, 346
escape:
- not to escape xxviii
- as an escape 531
restless, irritable & discontented xxvi
reasons for sobriety:
for people, places & things 187, 344
for yourself 98, 112, 379
just not to drink 192, 383,
(see also:sobriety is enough)

R

rebel 56, 94
receptive 91, 158
reconstruction .... (see:disease-tertiary care)
recover:
    recovered .... tp, xiii, xxiii, 17, 20, 90, 96, 132, 133, 146
    recovering .... f104(3rd ed.), 122
recovery .... (see also:subject matter)
    chance (of/for) 73, 96, 97, 120, 145
    essentials of .... 570, (see also:essentials)
    path to xxii
    plan of xxiii
    program of .... (see:program)
recovery:
    job or no job 98
    not dependent upon people 100
    permanent recovery .... xvii, (see also:permanent)
    regardless of anyone 98
    yourself .... (see:reasons for sobriety)
rectify - errors of the past .... (see:housecleaning)
reed 28
rehabilitation .... (see:disease-tertiary care)
relapse:
    anything is preferable to that 130
    it is by no means a bad thing 120
relapse .... (see also:disease-chronic,penality,repeat)
    bender 5, 23, 139, 142, 155
    binge 90, 112

R

relapse (cont'd):
- bout 23, 32, 90, 109, 140
- bust 138
- fall 73
- outburst 105
- spree .... xxvii, 21, 32, 35, 37, 73, 90, 92, 95, 106, 109, 113, 143, 155, 159

relationship with God .... (see:God-relationship)

relationship with newcomers 89, 100
- fellow 95
- friend 95, 152
- spiritual advisor 63
- sponsor 472, 494, 550

release .... (see also:bondage,free, freedom,permanent,struggles)
- by alcohol .... 151, 154, (see also:subtle foe)
- from alcoholism 55, 152, 159, 169, 189, 191, 208, 219
- from frustrations 128
- spiritual release 55

reliance .... (see:God-relationship)

reliance upon things human .... xxvi, (see also:human resources)

relief .... (see:disease-secondary care)

religion/religious .... (see also:anti-religious, prejudice,right)
- discussion of matters...religious 19
- has much in common with 131-132

religion/religious (cont'd):
- inquiry by...religious societies ... xiv
- organized religion ... 49
- religious experiences ... 569, (see also:spiritual...)
- simple religious idea ... 9, (see also:ideas,simple)
- we have gone religious ... 49

religious ... xiv, (see also:no opinion...)
- affiliations ... 28
- backgrounds ... 17
- bodies ... 28, 87
- connection ... 74
- convictions ... 27, 93
- denomination ... xiv, 74, 87, 93-94
- education & training ... 93
- faith ... 94
- leanings ... 90
- sect ... xiv

remedy ... (see:message)

remorse ... 6, 66, 81, 83, 86, 106, (see also:judgement,resentment, self-pity)

repair - the damage ... (see:housecleaning)

reparation ... (see:housecleaning)

repeat ... (see also:disease-chronic,relapse)
- over and over ... xxvii
- repeated stumbling ... 113

R

repeat (cont'd):
repitition 120
    setting the terrible cycle in motion 23
    time after time 35, 72
reprieve ..... (see:daily reprieve)
required xxvii
requirements ..... (see also:condition)
    essential requirements 14,
    (see also:essentials)
    first requirement - sanity 60,
    (see also:Step 3)
    only requirement for membership ..... xiv,
    (see also:relief)
    simple requirements 50,
    (see also:essentials,simple)
requires ..... xxvi, 25
resentment ..... (see also:block,judgement, rancor,remorse,sensitiveness)
    deadly hazard 117
    festering mental attitude 560
    grudge list 65
    harboring feelings - definition of 66
    number one offender 64
    prayer - to get rid of ..... (see:prayer-resentment)
    taking it personally 66
reservations ..... (see:convinced)
respect 19, 43,
    (see also:tolerance)

responsibility 154,
(see also:behavior,blame, conduct,past)
  for ourselves 473
  for the past:
    - actions are partly responsible 83
    - did much to make them so 127
    - knows he is to blame 123
    - of our own making 62, 103
    - we make our own misery 133
    - we...set the ball rolling 67
  for treatment 143
restitution .... (see:housecleaning)
restless, irritable & discontented .... xxvi,
(see also:reasons for drinking)
result:
  before considering the result 140
  commenced to get results 46
  getting results from this book xiv
  marvelous results 134,
  (see also:promises)
  much good will result 19
  result was nil 58
  results rather than methods 144,
  (see also:theory)
  stickler for facts and results 48
retaliate 61, 62, 67, 105
revealed 48
revelation 57, 309

R

riddle 22, 116,
(see also:humility,questions)

ridicule .... (see:judgement)

right .... (see also:prayer,proper,wrongs)

- perhaps they were right 3
- relationship with Him is right 164
- religious people are/were right 11, 87,
  (see also:religion/religious)
- right all such matters 13,
  (see also:wrongs)
- right answer 69, 86
- right ideal 70
- right kind of man 149
- right minds .... (see:sanity)
- right person 74
- right thing 97
- right thought or action 87
- right track 100,
  (see also:off/on)
- rightly and naturally 74

right - have no right 74, 81

right - having just claim to 80, 108, 115

right away .... (see:urgency)

right then .... (see:urgency)

rights & society .... (see:society)

risks .... (see:any lengths/extreme)

road of happy destiny 164,
(see also:path)

R

rocky road.. 104, 334
rule(s)..xix, xxvii, 74, 101, 118, 569,
(see also:Twelve Steps)
rummy.. 302, 423

S

sanity .... (see also:requirements,sobriety)
ceased fighting 84, 103
definition of 37
pray for 70,
(see also:prayer-ask for)
restored 57, 59, 285
returned 84, 154
right minds 57,
(see also:right)
sanity versus sobriety 463,
(see also:sobriety is enough)
third promise 83-84
salvation 220, 272
scoff .... xxx, 3
scrap heap .... (see:bottom)
seed has been planted 113, 117
self .... (see:convinced)
bondage of self 63,
(see also:prayer-Step 3)
decisions based on self 62
getting rid of self 62
his better self 108
infinite God...finite selves 68
self...was what had defeated us 64
threats to self (5 of them) 65-66
selfishness 62
self-appraisal .... (see:thinking)
self-centeredness 14, 61, 62, 124
self-confident 40, 68

S

self-conscious 115
self-control 26
self-deception 31,
(see also:denial)
    deceive 142
    delusion/self-delusion 30, 61, 62
    fooling ourselves 55, 152
    illusion 30
self-destruction 56
self-delusion .... (see:self-deception)
self-discipline 32, 569
self-esteem 64, 65,
(see also:threats to self)
self-evident 9,
(see also:faith-idea of)
self-imposed 53,
(see also:blame,responsibility)
self-knowledge 7, 39, 40
self-pity 8, 15, 61, 62, 84, 86,
88, 104, 105, 116, 127
self-propulsion 60
self-reliance .... xxix, 68,
(see also:human resources)
self-revealing 29,
(see also:authentication)
self-sacrificing 61, 93, 105
self-searching 25
self-seeker 61, 67
self-seeking 84, 86

S

self-sufficiency 52, 249,
(see also:human resources)
self-will 60, 62, 71, 76, 87,
(see also:block)
sensitiveness .... (see also:handicaps)
gossip 125
stick to your own story 92, 125,
taking each other's inventories 245,
(see also:fellowship-early AA)
serenity 68, 84,
(see also:peace)
service .... (see also:purpose, work)
benefit others 84,
(see also:past,promises)
giving versus getting 102, 128, 159,
(see also:action-attitude)
helpful .... xiv, 20, 89, 94, 95, 100, 162
helping others 70, 90, 97, 99, 164,
(see also:foundation stone)
kindness 67, 86
need - to be useful 156
needs of others 20, 70, 131
welfare of others 94, 161, 507
service plane .... (see also:dependence,plane)
sex .... (see also:girl who...,personal affairs)
amends 69-70, 124
comments on 68, 134
impotence 134

S

sharing .... (see:authentication)
shipwreck analogy .... (see:desperation)
shortcomings 59,
(see also:defects,flaws,off/on,prejudice)
prayer for .... (see:prayer-Step 7)
tolerance of 103,
(see also:tolerance)
sick .... xii, 18, 66, 67, 70, 100, 101,
106, 107, 108, 115, 130, 141
simple:
at a simpler level 47
elements...are simple 57,
(see also:essentials,fundamentals)
simple, but not easy 14
and personal xxii
and understandable 28
attitude 27
cornerstone 47,
(see also:arch)
good ideas 62
kit 25
matter - keeping sober 40
principles 130
program 58
reliance 52,
(see also:God-relationship)
religious idea 9,
(see also:ideas)

S

simple (cont'd):
requirements 50,
(see also:requirements)
rules .... xxvii,
(see also:twelve Steps)
steps 46,
(see also:twelve Steps)
talk 16,
(see also:self-revealing)
things 50
way 88
simply wish to be helpful xiv
sinful/sins 13, 61, 135
six steps 292
skid row .... (see:bottom)
slander 80
sleeping .... (see:phobias)
slip .... (see:disease-chronic)
sobriety .... xvii, 32, 33, 100, 101, 119,
128, 129, 146, 152,
(see also:Step 12)
emotional 452,
(see also:sanity)
success 447, 525
taking credit for .... (see:ego)
sobriety 447, 463
he owes you more than sobriety 118
sobriety is enough 82
social distinctions .... (see:fellowship)

society 11, 26, 62,
(see also:life,useful/ness)
social life of this world 102
society & rights 549
trusted citizen 80
vital place 15
solution .... (see:message)
Spirit .... (see:God-titles of)
spiritual .... (see also:change)
awakening 47, 381, 417, 569
experience 14, 25, 27, 28, 42, 44, 46,
128, 130, 157, 569
transformation 143, 569
spiritual experience:
experience versus awakening 381, 569
maintenance & growth of 66, 84,
(see also:growth)
spiritual experience - attributes .... (see also:vital)
dramatic 55
extraordinary 28
overwhelming 56
powerful 113, 130
profound 14
revolutionary 50
spectacular 113
stirring 128
sudden 14, 27
sudden & spectacular 569

S

spiritual principles....42, 60, 93, 97, 116, 130, 139, 156, (see also:principles)
spiritual structure....(see:arch)
spiritual tools....25, 95
spiritually fit....85, 101, (see also:neutrality)
sponsor....(see:relationship with newcomers)
spree....(see:relapse)
stability....49
state of the nations(s)....61, 132
stealing....6, 68
Step 1....59, 379-380, 471
Step 3....(see also:let go)
  care of....59
  care & direction of....13, 158
  first requirement....(see:requirements)
  prayer....(see:prayer-Step 3)
Step 12 - benefits of:
  he may be helping you more than you are helping him....94
  insure his sobriety....129
  insure immunity from drinking....89
  to maintain his sobriety....119, 146
Step 12 - calls....60,
  carry another "fellow"....185, 206, 216
  carry the Big Book....90, 92, 94, 95
  carry a bottle....102, 206, 207
  carry this/a beneficial message....60, 77, 89, (see also:message)

Step 12 - calls (cont'd)
get background information ... 90
see your man alone ... 91
Step 12 - purpose ... (see also:handicapped, purpose of individual)
opportunity/chance - for AA member ... 67, 138
opportunity/chance - for prospect ... 19, 90, 96, 114, 147, 148, 164
that needs it & wants it ... 186
willing & able to get well/recover ... 97, 162
Step 12 - attitude of tough love:
drop him ... 95
firm attitude ... 142
if he means business ... 114, 147, 161
waste of time - on prospect ... 90, 96, 142, 186, (see also:either/or)
Steps (n1):
the first Step in recovery ... 30
we were at Step Three ... 60
This was Step Four ... 64
the Fifth Step ... 72
Step Six ... 76
Step Seven ... 76
Steps Eight and Nine ... 76
Step Ten ... 84
Step Eleven ... 85
Step Twelve ... 88
stop drinking ... (see:quit)

S

story ....29, 36, 43, 55, 73, 74, 75, 80, 91, 125, (see also:authentication,self-revealing)
stories - personal stories....................29, 52, 165
straighten:
out the past.................... (see:past)
set these matters straight.................... 67
straighten out 64
stream:
of life.................... 86
of misery.................... 163
struggles:
other than drinking ....xvii, 16, 86, 118
to stop drinking 92
stubbornness.................... 140, (see also:obstinacy)
stumble ....(see:disease-chronic)
subject:
in these pages....................xxv
let him bring up the subject 111
no matter what the subject .... 118, (see also:no matter what)
of drinking 114
ought to know the subject better.................... 112
presented in this book....................xxv

(n1) The word "Step" and the number of the Step are all capitalized except for the first Step reference. There is no explicit reference to Step Two.

S

subject matter - of this book....xxv, 143,
(see also:recovery)
arrested....311, 480
cure(d)....85, 118, 135, 138, 180, 188, 191,
(see also:daily/day,ex-)
solved....17
subject of God....45, 77,
(see also:God-relationship with)
submit....(see:surrender)
substitute....152,
(see also:fellowship)
success....xvii, 60, 95
first principle of....111,
(see also:anger,principles)
material/financial....2, 3, 127, 507
not drinking....34, 447
skid row of success....345,
(see also:bottom)
success & failure....525
succumbed....(see:surrender)
suffer....xxiii, 17, 22, 23, 24,
109, 114, 124, 155, 159, 573
suggestions/suggestive....86, 87, 130, 132, 143, 148, 164
sunlight:
stood in the sunlight....12
sunlight of the spirit....66
superiority - intellectual....343, 400, 412, 533, 537,
(see also:ego)
Supreme Being....(see:God-titles of)

S

surrender........186, 271, 340, 503,
(see also:ideas-old,our, let go)
abandon........15, 45, 48, 59, 63, 164
accept........xvi, xxv, 25, 39, 47, 48, 143
admit:
- defeat/drinking........xxvi, 11 13, 59, 92, 110
- faults/shortcomings........67, 72, 81, 99, 127
cannot subscribe........133,
(see also:cannot or will not)
capitulated........160
concede:
- defeat/drinking........30, 40, 155
- faults/shortcomings........122
submit to anything to get well........142
succumbed........160
sweets........133,
(see also:craving,health)

T

takes us out of ourselves 70,
(see also:service,Step 12)
teetotaler 139,
(see:Sect.III-ppt)
telephone:
calls saying he is sick 146
insisted on speaking with me 136
interrupted by the telephone 8
phone a clergyman 154
telephone had never been invented 115
telephone may jangle 97
woman's voice...long distance 137
temperance:
pledge 10
society 572
temperament .... (see:mental attitude)
temptation 85,
(see also:neutrality)
cause of 507
craving for/compulsion 181, 285
desire to drink 219
shield from 101, 120, 147
taste for liquor 259
thought of a drink 57
tenets:
of the Oxford Groups .... (see:Sect.III-ppt)
totally honest 482
tendencies .... (see:mental attitude)
testimony .... (see:authentication)

T

text ....xi, f155(3rd ed.), 381
thankful 127,
(see also:gratitude,resentment)
theory.................... (see also:experience,practical)
doctor's theory xxiv
spiritual life is not a theory 83
we are not theorizing 70
thinking 13, 24, 53, 86, 87, 114, 140,
(see also:motives,prayer-ask for)
analysis....................55, 70, 83, 104, 546
charity, when justified....................(see:dependence)
consequences 37, 107,
(see also:consequences,any lengths...)
considered it carefully 65
cleared of wrong motives 86
impulsive & undisciplined....................37, 62, 88, 256, 325
made clear distinction 44
self-appraisal....................72, 76, 94
thought well...this Step 63
unthinking 82, 107,
(see also:sobriety is enough)
use discretion 96
ways of thinking.................... 50, 118
we think well before we choose 74
tidings ....(see:message)
time:
long period of reconstruction 83
long time to repair.................... 127
one year.................... 34

time (cont'd):
six months 141
year and a half 15
years 123
time .... (see also:growth,patience)
for reconstruction 83, 99, 123, 127
remaining dry .... (see:one year)
taking the Steps .... (see:urgency)
to clear away the wreck .... 123, (see also:wreck)
to drink is to die .... 15, 66, 457, (see also:convinced,death)
today, tomorrow or the hereafter .... 63, (see also:yesterday)
tolerance .... 19, 67, 70, 84 (see also:Live And Let Live, patience,shortcomings)
tools .... (see:spiritual tools)
traits .... 61, 92, (see also:earmarks)
transformation .... 133, 143, (see also:spiritual...)
treatment .... xxiii, 26, 30, 143, (see also:responsibility)
troubles .... (see also:bedevilments,problem)
domestic .... (see:past)
of our own making .... 62, (see also:responsibility)
root of .... 62, (see also:selfishness)

T

true alcoholic ....(see:alcoholic)
trust in God & clean house 98,
(see also:housecleaning,condition)
truth 23, 64, 71, 144
turn in all things 14
turning point 59,
(see also:bottom)
Twelve Steps .... xxii, 96,
(see also:program,six steps)
directions 29, 85
instructions 185
proposals 75
rules .... xxvi,
(see also:rules,simple)
suggestions 59, 89
twenty four hours .... (see:daily/day)
two fold nature .... (see:disease...)
twos and threes and fives .... (see:fellowship-early AA)

U

understanding/confidence .... (see also:common ground)
  know/knew what...talking about 18, 94, 180, 189
  with the fellowship 228, 312, 355
  understanding - by others 18, 112, 122, 127
unmindful 10, 11, 25
urgency .... (see also:postpone,time)
  at once .... xxvii, 64, 84, 86, 92, 95, 96, 113, 117
  don't delay 83
  immediate(ly) 84, 99, 569
  instantly 123
  now 59
  promptly 64
  quickly 31, 84
  right away 120
  right then 11
  sudden(ly) .... (see:spiritual experience-atttributes)
  waste no time 75
ups & downs .... 117, (see also:roller coaster)
useful/-ness .... (see also:affairs,service)
  useful/-ness 8, 20, 43, 49, 76, 130, 132, 153, 156, 158
  useful program .... 19, (see also:program)
utmost:
  do our utmost 19
  doing his utmost 147
  done our utmost 77

U

utmost (cont'd):
manage with the utmost assurance 1
to the utmost of my ability 13
utmost frankness 82
Utopia 16, 6l,
(see also:heaven,hereafter)

V

vanity .... (see:ego)
vicarious pleasure 101
vicissitude 56
victory & defeat:
alcohol is a subtle foe 85
conquer 44, 98
defeated - by self 11, 42, 64, 113, 153
enemies .... (see:greatest enemies)
generalship 82
victory
- over (my difficulties) 63
- over alcohol 76
- over hurt pride 125
- sense of victory 14
viewpoints .... (see:mental attitude)
violent 35, 91, 97, 110
virtually:
no other solution .... (see:monopoly)
impossible for him to stop 22-23,
(see also:control,impossible)
vital .... xvii, 15, 27, 64, 72, 85, 93, 94

W

Wallace Beery movies.......... 177, 441
wants & needs.......... (see:needs)
waste of time.......... 87, 148,
(see also:Step 12-attitude)
watchwords.......... 118,
(see also:common ground)
way of life/living.......... (see:life)
we are not saints.......... 60,
(see also:growth)
welfare - of others.......... (see:service)
well.......... (see also:free,recover)
get well.......... 85, 97-98, 98, 142, 147, 154
got well.......... 93, 110
have seen men get well.......... 100
six months later, a well man.......... 141
well - other than recovery.......... 6, 8, 21, 63, 74,
78, 126, 129, 139
well-being.......... 127, 137, 149
wet brain.......... 7,
(see also:alternatives)
What do I have to do?.......... 20,
(see also:purpose-of book)
what's the use anyhow?.......... 24
what we used to be like, what
happened, and what we are like now.......... 58,
(see also:drunk-a-log)
why:
first drink.......... 35,
(see also:insanity)
he should believe.......... 48

why (cont'd):
we were angry 64,
(see also:threats to self)
why me? 22, 380,
(see also:riddle)
why was this? - lack of control 26,
will
(see also:purpose)
bidding 76
dictates 100
play the role He assigns 68,
(see also:actor,play)
proper use of 85
self will .... (see:self-will)
Thy will 63, 67, 85, 88,
(see also:App.7)
will power .... (see:human resources)
willing & able .... (see:Step 12-purpose)
willing(ness) .... (see also:essentials, HOW)
I'll do anything .... (see:desperation)
receptivity 94, 96, 163
to believe 12, 46, 47, 53, 93
to make amends 69-70, 124, 503
to work the program 13, 76, 124
willingness .... (see also:convinced)
cannot or will not 16, 58, 96, 114, 148,
(see also:blind)
could not or would not .... (see:blind)
unwilling to admit .... xxviii, 30, 93,
(see also:denial)

W

witchburners .... (see:pass it on-how not to)
witness .... (see:authentication)
wives - finest 81, 82, 105, 178
work 15, 19, 84, 93, 95,
(see also:faith without...,service)
alcoholic work xiii
avocation xiii
effort 26, 64
labor 163
on a service plane 98,
(see also:charity,plane)
persist 100
sole vocation 19
strenuous xvii
trudge 164
with another alcoholic 89, 102,
(see also:service,Step 12)
with others 14-15, 70, 119
worst day sober, best day drunk 11, 43,
(see also:life-old life)
wreck .... (see also:past)
time to clear away the wreck 123
wreckage of your past 164
wringer 38, 43, 243
(see also:bottom)
wrongs 13, 56, 66, 67, 129, 135,
(see also:housecleaning)
wrong motives 86,
(see also:thinking)
wrong-doing .... (see:housecleaning)

X, Y, Z

APPENDIX 1

THE DISEASE MODEL

Although the word "disease" is used only once - on page 64 as a "spiritual disease" - thru page 164 of the Big Book, there is an emerging consensus to classify alcoholism as a disease by members of the fellowship and workers in the field of alcoholism.

The reluctance of Bill W. to use the term "disease" was reinforced in 1951 by the American Public Health Association which emphasized alcoholism as an illness and again in 1957 by the American Medical Association which officially declared alcoholism to be a "highly complex illness".

In essence, although many have come to regard alcoholism as a specific disease entity, there is yet no precise agreement about what it means to say that alcoholism is a disease. This is probably the major factor in using the non-specific label of "illness" rather than the specific designation of "disease".

Although this concordance takes no position as to the validity of the disease model as a descriptor, the model does offer a convenient, comprehensive and easily understood frame of reference for classifying the various aspects of this complex illness. Hence, this concordance employs the disease model concept.

It should be emphasized that the disease model approach was not selected to create a seething caldron of debate nor provoke heated argument. If this scheme promotes useful discussion, fine. The final verdict has not yet been reached.

disease - etiology........(see:problem,troubles)
disease - spiritual........64,
(see also:alcoholism as...)
disease - biological onset........(see also:impunity, neutrality)
immunity........33, 89, 181,
(see also:neutrality)
which came first - nature or nuture........240
disease - pathological onset........(see also:riddle)
at some stage........21,
(see also:control)
body...as abnormal as his mind........xxiv
bodily and mentally different........22, 30
no such thing as making a normal
drinker out of an alcoholic........31
once a certain point is reached........22
power of choice........(see:choice)
disease - clinical onset:
signs & symptoms........32, 33, 38, 67, 91, 138
of a deeper trouble........64, 103, 544
(see also:causes&conditions)
the symptom........xxviii, 44,
(see also:control,craving)

APPENDIX 2

"I'LL DO ANYTHING"

The phrase "I'll do anything" is a cry of absolute desperation and despair that only an alcoholic of the hopeless variety (the "real" alcoholic or "true" alcoholic) utters when he or she finally surrenders. This cry is a recognition of the willingness to go to "any lengths" or "any extreme" in order to be released from the bondage of alcoholism.

As the "mental states that preceed a relapse into drinking is the crux of the problem" (page 35), the degree of willingness often has to be maintained for some time after the prospect is no longer jittery or befogged. Perhaps the clearest and most direct statement of this complete willingness to "do anything" is found in the story "Hindsight" which appears in the first edition of the Big Book on pages 370 through 374. On page 373, the author writes:

> "When I decided to do something about my problem, I was reconciled to the fact that it might be necessary for me to wash dishes, scrub floors, or do some menial task for possibly many years in order to re-establish myself as a sober, sane and reliable person."

APPENDIX 3

MAN ON THE BED

Originally titled: "Came to Believe...", this full-color painting was created by the artist Robert M. (a member of the fellowship) who was a volunteer illustrator for the "A.A. Grapevine" monthly magazine.

A replica of the painting first appeared under the caption: "Came To Believe..." as a center spread in the December, 1955 issue (vol. 12, no. 7) of the "A.A. Grapevine". In May of 1956, Robert M. presented the original painting as a gift to Bill W. (a co-founder of Alcoholics Anonymous). Bill W. wrote a thank you letter to Robert M. and referred to the painting as a representation of a "man on the bed".

The title of the painting was changed from "Came To Believe..." to "Man On the Bed" when Alcoholics Anonymous World Services, Inc. published the book: Came to Believe... in 1973.

According to the Editors of the Big Book, the three men depicted in the painting were to represent the first "twelth step call". On page 188, two men were identified as:

Bill D. - the man on the bed,
Bill W. - the man who sat by the side of the bed.

Therefore: Dr. Bob - the man who sat by the dresser.

APPENDIX 4

"MUST"

A dictionary defines the word "must" as: (1) a compulsion or obligation, (2) an absolute requirement; unavoidable responsibility and (3) absolutely necessary.

The "must" listed below are listed in page number order rather than alphabetical order.

1) do likewise xxiii
2) believe xxiv
3) have depth xxvi
4) be grounded in a power xxvi
5) stop drinking xxvii
6) help xxvii
7) feel xxvii
8) admit xxvii
9) listen 10
10) turn in all things 14
11) be weak 20
12) have this thing 29
13) be no reservations 33
14) come from a higher power 43
15) find a spiritual basis 44
16) be rid of this selfishness 62
17) or it kills us 62

18) be mastered.......... 66
19) be willing.......... 69
20) make amends.......... 69
21) be entirely honest.......... 73
22) confess.......... 74
23) be hard on ourselves.......... 74
24) not...postpone.......... 75
25) lose our fear.......... 78
26) not shrink at anything.......... 79
27) not shrink.......... 80
28) say.......... 81
29) keep sober.......... 82
30) take the lead.......... 83
31) remember.......... 83
32) carry the vision.......... 85
33) go with us.......... 85
34) go further.......... 85
35) be careful.......... 86
36) not miss.......... 89
37) decide these things.......... 90
38) be accompanied by action.......... 93
39) decide for himself.......... 95
40) come from within.......... 95
41) be done.......... 99
42) try to repair the damage.......... 99
43) be on a better basis.......... 99
44) walk in the path.......... 100
45) not go where liquor is served.......... 100
46) not have it.......... 101

47) shun friends 101
48) avoid moving pictures 101
49) not go into bars 101
50) hide their bottles 101
51) think or be reminded 101
52) do about his drinking 111
53) act 113
54) start life anew 114
55) be on guard 115
56) apologize 115
57) carry the burden 117
58) not expect 118
59) redouble 120
60) realize 127
61) see the danger 127
62) remember 127
63) be done 130
64) be convinced 135
65) stop 141
66) change 143
67) abide 144
68) decide 144
69) be honest 146
70) get along without liquor 152
71) find a way out 153
72) be many such 154
73) keep spiritually active 156
74) help other alcoholics 159
75) remember 164

76)	work together	563
77)	continue to live	565
78)	be in the nature of	569
79)	must acquire	569
80)	take...cognizance of	571
81)	merit consideration	571
82)	never drink	572

In addition to the explicit "musts", there are several implicit "musts". The first one is the word "imperative" which is connected to "must" by the common word "obligation". The second one is the set of colloquialisms: "had better", "had to", "has to" and "have to" which are used to express obligation or necessity. The reader is directed to the main body of this concordance for these implied "musts".

	Forewords				text		
	1st	2nd	3rd	D.O.	1-164	App.	Total
had better	0	0	0	0	3	0	3
had to	0	2	0	0	12	0	14
has to	0	0	0	0	3	0	3
have to	0	0	0	0	4	0	4
imperative	0	0	0	1	2	0	3
must	0	1	0	7	60	6	74
must never / must not	0	0	0	0	7	1	8

Legend: D.O. = The Doctor's Opinion

APPENDIX 5

"OFF THE BEAM" / "ON THE BEAM"

To be "on the beam" is an expression that comes from the use of a now obsolete aerial navigation aid called the VAR (visual-aural, A-N, range) system. This system beamed directional radio signals to an airplane, thus enabling the pilot fly an identifiable, pre-set course between two airports. If the pilot was flying "on the beam" then he was said to be "right on course". Slang equivalents such as "right track", "correct course", "good path" and others, are used to signify acceptance and/or approval of the actions of individuals or groups. For example, an individual's regard for himself may be termed conceit or self esteem, depending on whether or not another person approves of it.

The phrases "off the beam" and "on the beam" refer to the practice of the tenth step. Each phrase represents a list of character attributes that serve as guidelines for a daily moral inventory.

The phrase "off the beam" is a figurative expression used to signify the departure from a usual or prescribed course. It stands for a list of twelve character defects and shortcomings. In this concordance, the traits listed can be found under the keywords: anger, bondage, contention, ego, enemies, prejudice and selfishness. This expression appears in the story "Promoted to Chronic" on page 491 of the second edition and on page 471 of the third edition. The equivalent expressions "off the track" and "on the wrong track" are found on pages 68 and 98 respectively.

The phrase "on the beam" is a figurative expression used to denote adherence to a usual or perscribed course. It stands for a list of twelve character assets or virtues. This expression does not appear in the Big Book but an equivalent one "on the right track" is found on page 100.

	OFF THE BEAM	ON THE BEAM
1.	fear	faith
2.	worry	hope
3.	anger	generosity-charity
4.	jealousy	aspiration
5.	criticism	patience
6.	vanity	sympathy
7.	hatred	non-interference
8.	envy	kindness
9.	hypocrisy	courage
10.	prejudice	forgiveness
11.	selfishness	duty
12.	greed	love

The popularity and usage of these guidelines has diminished since the decade of the 40's, but they can still be found hanging on the walls of some "older" clubrooms and meeting halls and especially those which are located in the southeast and southwest regions of the country.

APPENDIX 6

THE PROMISES

The promises of Alcoholics Anonymous (pages 83-84) are the solution to the bedevilments (page 52). Since there are twelve steps, twelve traditions and twelve concepts for world service, attempts have been made to order and number the promises in order to construct twelve promises.

One such attempt takes the phrase: "we will be amazed before we are half way through" as the first promise. Combined with the next eleven sentences, twelve promises appear.

Another attempt is to list the first promise: "we are going to know a new freedom and a new happiness" and then split the third promise:

"we will comprehend the word serenity

and we will know peace"

at the word "and" and thereby construct two promises:

"we will comprehend the word serenity"

and "we will know peace"

Again, the result is the construction of twelve promises.

The promises are not numbered in the Big Book. To avoid argument and controversy, promises beyond number three are not referenced by a number in this concordance. Hence, the "last" promise (whether number eleven or twelve) is: "we will suddenly realize that God is doing for us what we could not do for ourselves."

Although there is insufficient evidence at present to support a definite conclusion, the effort to construct the "Twelve Promises" may also have been influenced by the construction of the twelve items in the "On The Beam" and "Off The Beam" lists (see Appendix 5). Evidently, there exists a strong attraction with the number twelve.

APPENDIX 7

God and pronouns for God

The two lists below tabulate references to the word "God" and the pronouns for God such as "He", "Him", "His", etc., thru page 164 of the Big Book and the appendices to the Big Book. The number within parentheses represents the number of times the word "God" or pronoun can be found on the indicated page.

The word "God" is mentioned one hundred and thirty two (132) times and pronouns for "God" are mentioned eighty (80) times.

GOD:

xvi (1);	10 (1);	12 (5);	13 (3);	14 (1);
24 (1);	25 (2);	28 (2);	29 (1);	45 (4);
46 (3);	47 (3);	49 (2);	51 (2);	53 (1);
54 (1);	55 (3);	56 (3);	57 (2);	59 (5);
60 (1);	62 (4);	63 (2);	67 (3);	68 (4);
69 (4);	70 (2);	71 (1);	72 (1);	75 (1);
76 (2);	77 (2);	80 (2);	81 (1);	83 (1);
84 (2);	85 (2);	86 (4);	87 (1);	88 (1);
93 (1);	95 (1);	98 (3);	100 (2);	114 (1);
116 (3);	117 (1);	120 (2);	121 (1);	123 (1);
124 (1);	128 (4);	129 (1);	130 (1);	133 (4);
155 (1);	156 (1);	158 (4);	161 (1);	162 (1);
164 (5);	564 (1);	565 (1);	569 (1);	570 (1);

PRONOUNS

11 (2);	12 (5);	13 (5);	14 (1);	45 (1);
53 (2);	55 (3);	57 (5);	59 (5);	60 (2);
62 (5);	63(12);	67 (1);	68 (8);	71 (1);
75 (1);	76 (1);	85 (4);	88 (1);	116 (1);
120(1);	130 (2);	133 (1);	158 (1);	164 (4);
564(2);	565 (2);	568 (1).		

SECTION II

MOTTOES, SLOGANS & TERMS

INTRODUCTION

A motto or slogan is a concisely expressed principle of behavior or rule of conduct that has been drawn from practical experience. It is a simple and direct expression of wisdom that is well worn by repetition. The six mottoes or slogans often seen hanging in meeting room and on clubhouse walls are:

But for The Grace of God

Easy Does It (But Do It)

First Things First

Let Go and Let God

Live and Let Live

Think, Think, Think

The phrase written in the parentheses above is an extension of the motto "Easy Does It". When "Easy Does It" is spoken, there is usually a pause, followed by "But Do It" in a lowered and measured voice to emphasize the importance of taking action. The purpose of this "add-on" is to avoid the tendency to postpone (procrastinate) working the program. Falling into the trap that "Easy Does It" can often lead to "not doing it" has its consequences. As one member who achieved sobriety in the mid 40's states on page 471: "But the older members in A.A. told me 'Easy Does It'. In the light of subsequent events it became evident that I took their advice far too literally, for, after some months of happy sobriety I drank again."

All but the last of the six mottoes are direct extractions from the Big Book. This last motto is an apparent contradiction with the often used injunction:

Utilize, Don't Analyse

because the underlying, implicitly understood, but unstated Fellowship philosophy can be summarized as: "you don't have to think or understand it, just accept it and be grateful that it works".

In the Fellowship, many mottoes and slogans have been popularly accepted over the years because "older" members have found them useful in their own recovery and have passed them on by sharing their own experience, strength and hope.

DOUBLE QUESTION MARKS (??)

The set of double question marks within a set of parenthesis and catenated to the right of a main entry is used to denote an idea or concept that seemingly constitutes a departure from the traditional AA program. It is ignored in the collating sequence.

EARLIER EDITIONS

There are many expressions one hears at meetings which do not appear in the third edition of the Big Book. The sayings which are present in the first and second editions and which are still frequently used are listed below along with the page number(s) for each edition.

The First Edition:

business of living 219
can't stand prosperity 348
eye openers 219
God looks after drunken
fools & little children 244, 371
hair of the dog that bit you 219, 254
religionist 199

The Second Edition:

AA doesn't need me but I need AA 507
bottom of the barrel 502
ex-drunks 452
grandiosity 339
lower companionship 371
one drink away from a drunk 438
reading my mail 371
Sally (Salvation Army) 502
that should qualify me 445

MOTTOES, SLOGANS AND TERMS

On page 25 the Big Book refers to the "simple kit of spiritual tools". One of the major sets of tools in the kit is the set of mottoes, slogans and aphorisms. Below is a recapitulation of the mottoes and slogans that are currently in vogue and which also appear in this work. This list is not exhaustive as the Fellowship is ever changing and therefore the tools that are used find ever different forms of expression. Note that the cross references that appear in this listing may be found in the Concordance.

ABC's 60,
(see also:Sect.III-changes...,ideas)
allergic reaction 213, 246
attitude of gratitude .... (see:grace...)
bankrupt .... (see:bottom, skid row)
cafeteria style 11, 273
character assassination .... (see:slander)
civilians .... (see:normal folks/people)
earth people .... (see:normal folks/people)
excuses/"reasons" .... (see also:fallacious reasoning)
  if only .... (see:recovery)
  only if - if you had 439-441
for free & for fun .... (see:action-attitude,grace...-gift)
geographic cure 4, 281, 358, 522
Great Discovery .... (see:God-discovery of)
gut-level acceptance .... (see:deep)
honesty - levels of:
  cash-register honesty .... (see:money,stealing)
  honesty with others .... (see:honest,slander)
  self-honesty .... (see:honest)
identification .... (see:understanding/confidence)
I want what I want when I want it .... (see:self, selfishness)
it's an inside job .... (see:deep)
Keep An Open Mind .... (see:essentials)

MOTTOES, SLOGANS & TERMS

Keep Coming Back........415
Keep It Simple........(see:simple)
Keep It Simple Stupid(??)........(see:simple)
Let Go and Let God........(see:let go)
living problem........29, 40, 52, 55, 87, 90, 160,
(see also:bedevilments,leaving aside...)
locked up, covered up or sobered up........(see:alternatives)
message, not the messenger........(see also:dependence, faith in...)
slips........271
sponsor of my sponsor........245
no pain, no gain........(see:past,growth)
normies........(see:normal folks/people)
occupational therapy........445,
(see also:ego-pride)
One Day At A Time........340
(see also:daily/day)
people, places & things........(see also:faith in...)
pink cloud........348
pitch........(see:drunk-a-log,what we...)
pity pot........(see:self-pity)
playpens & playmates - change your(??)........101-102
priorities........(see:First Things First)
put the plug in the jug........(see:disease-secondary care)
qualify - as an alcoholic........(see:Sect.II-earlier editions)
resentment prayer........552,
(see also:prayer)
revolving door........(see:disease-primary care)

roller coaster 117, 127, 560
selfish program(??) 62, 159, 236,
surrender 186, 503
(see also:ideas-old,our, let go)
taking others inventories .... (see:fellowship-early AA, sensitiveness)
Think, Think, Think .... (see:thinking)
tough love .... (see:Step 12-attitude)
Turn It Over 280,
(see also:God's hands,let go)
twelve Step calls .... (see:Step 12-calls)
utilize, don't analyze(??) .... (see:thinking)
white knuckle 152, 339,
(see also:disease-secondary care)
works best for most .... (see:monopoly,virtually)

SECTION III

A GUIDE

CHANGES TO THE BIG BOOK

According to the Big Book, the "chief change" over the years has been the enlargement of the personal stories section to reflect the change and increase in membership. The following table provides an explicit accounting of the growth in the personal stories section.

edition	page	personal stories
manuscript	42	more than a score
first	39	more than a score(n2)
second	ffdc, 165	thirty-seven
	29	three dozen
third	ffdc, xii	forty-four
	29, 165	forty-three

(n2) The 1st pr. contained 29 stories. The story:"Lone Endeavor" appeared only in the 1st pr. Thus, all other printings contained 28 stories.

CHANGES TO THE BIG BOOK (cont'd)

The preface to the second edition states on page xi: "Therefore the first portion of this volume,..., has been left largely untouched." Likewise, the preface to the third edition states on page xi: "Therefore, the first portion of this volume,..., has been left untouched in the course..." However, there have been some changes made to the text over the years.

One such change is found in the wording of Step 12 in chapter 5. While a major rewording of this step ocurred in the transition from the manuscript edition to the first edition, another, more subtle, change ocurred in the transiton from the first edition to the second edition. The table below lists the changed wording of the twelfth step.

edition	page	Step 12
manuscript	24	this course of action
first	72	these steps (1st pr.)
	72	those steps (2nd-16th pr.)
second	60	these steps
third	60	these steps

CHANGES TO THE BIG BOOK (cont'd)

Another change is in the wording of the "C" in the "ABC's" - the three pertinent ideas - which appear in the beginning of chapter 5. The reader is directed to the table below which lists the changes in the wording of the third pertinent idea.

edition	page	the "C" of the "ABC's"
manuscript	24	that God can and will.
first	72	that God could and would if sought
second	60	that God could and would if He were sought.
third	60	that God could and would if He were sought.

CHANGES TO THE BIG BOOK (cont'd)

One final example of a textual change centers around the replacement of the word "hundreds" by the word "thousands" to reflect the growth in the Fellowship (e.g. title page and pages 17, 50, 113). The following four sentences appear on page 138 in the manuscript edition:

> "About a year ago, a certain state institution released six chronic alcoholics. It was fully expected they would all be back in a few weeks. Only one of them has returned. The others had no relapse at all.

These four sentences were replaced by the following two sentences which appear on page 127 of the first edition:

> "During 1939 two state hospitals in New Jersey released 17 alcoholics. Eleven have had no relapse whatever - none of them have returned to the asylum." (n3).

These two sentences were then replaced by the following single sentence which appears on page 114 in both the second and third editions:

> "Since this book was first published, A.A. has released thousands of alcoholics from asylums and hospitals of every kind."

(n3) The two state institutions above were the Greystone Psychiatric Hospital in Morris County near Morris Plains, NJ and Overbrook Asylum in Essex County, NJ.

EMPHASIS

The idea of emphasis is to lead the reader to see your ideas in the same relative importance in which you regard them. Emphasis does not necessarily mean force, but rather the accurate conveying of the writer's outlook and view of the subject. There are several ways in which emphasis can be conveyed.

A portion of text can be emphasised by use of: an appositive [and its asssociated em dash(s)], wording such as "Once more" (page 43), capital letters and/or italicized words, and exclamation points.

There are 46 exclamation points in the Big Book. The number within parentheses represents the number of times an exclamation point can be found on the indicated page.

EXCLAMATION POINTS:

xvii(4),	4(1),	6(1),	8(1),	9(4),	11(1),
12(1),	14(1),	24(1),	31(1),	34(1),	37(1),
54(2),	56(1),	57(1),	59(2),	60(1),	62(1),
63(1),	73(1),	85(1),	89(1),	100(1),	101(1),
102(1),	103(1),	106(1),	114(1),	116(2),	121(1),
123(1),	124(1),	128(1),	137(1),	151(1),	153(1),
154(1)					

VARIANTS

Many words may be spelled in more than one way. The variant used may be a matter of personal choice or it may be a local or regional convention.

For a compound word in which all the elements of the word can be written independently, the compound word may be variously written in a solid, open, or hyphenated form. The variants are known as variations of style. The following table lists some of the more conspicuous variations of style found in the Big Book. The number within the parenthesis refers to the page number(s) of the book in which the variation appears.

open form	hyphenated form
drawn out (278-2nd&3rd ed.)	drawn-out (333-1st ed.)
fair weather (122, 296)	fair-weather (3)
scrap heap (11, 542)	scrap-heap (296)
self discipline (569)	self-discipline (32)
self pity (376, 380)	self-pity (n4)
skid row (345, 379)	skid-row (319)

One instance was found where an expression appeared both in a solid form and an open form.

highroad (xvi)	high road (xxi-2nd ed.)

(n4) See the main body of the Concordance for a complete listing of page number references.

PEOPLE PLACES AND THINGS

page	reference	people places and things
tp	alcoholism	the term "alcoholism" was coined by Dr. Magnus Huss, a Swedish physician, in 1849.
xvi	tenets	The tenets of the Oxford Group are known as the "Four Absolutes" of Love, Honesty, Purity and Unselfishness.
xiii	well-known doctor	William Duncan Silkworth, M.D.
xvii	very first case	Their very first case was Eddie R. Their first successful case was Bill D. who became AA #3.
xxiii	chief physician	His actual title was 'Medical Director' at the time the letters of endorsement were written.
xxiii	nationally prominent hospital	Charles B. Towns Hospital, 293 Central Park West, New York, NY. It is now an apartment building.
xxix	a man	Henry P. See notes to the page 136 reference of "I was at one time..."
xxix	another case	Fitz M. See notes to the page 55 reference of "experience of a man"
2	night law course	at the Brooklyn Law School 250 Toralemon St., Brooklyn, NY.
3	Walter Hagen	A top professional golfer (1892 - 1969) who reached the apex of his career from 1914 to 1929. In 1921, he shot a then world record 18-hole

page	reference	people places and things
		score of 62. In 1926, he defeated Bobby Jones in match advertised as for the "world championship".
4	friend in Montreal	Dick Johnson
4	Elba & St. Helena	Napolean Bonaparte (1769-1821) was exiled to the island of Elba off the west coast of Italy. He escaped and returned to power. He was exiled again - permanently - to the island of st. Helena off the west coast of Africa after his defeat at the battle of Waterloo.
5	my wife's parents	Dr. Clark & Mrs. Burnham at 182 Clinton Street, Brooklyn Heights, New York.
7	brother-in-law	Dr. Leonard V. Strong, Jr.
7	nationally-known	Charles B. Towns Hospital.
7	belladonna treatment	Belladonna is the name of a sedative, antispasmodic drug that is extracted from the roots of the belladonna plant. The drug is used for the relief of muscle spasms, especially in the gastro-intestinal tract, due to nausea and diarrhea. The belladonna treatment was developed by the New York Physician Dr. Sam Lambert. It is no longer a standard medical treatment.

PEOPLE PLACES AND THINGS

page	reference	people places and things
7	kind doctor	William Duncan Silkworth, M.D.
8	old school friend	Edwin "Ebby" Thatcher. Sober in August, 1934. Bill W. looked upon Ebby as his sponsor.
8	Armistice Day	A holiday celebrated on Nov. 11th from 1919 to 1971 to commemorate the end of World War I on Nov 11, 1918. Renamed "Veteran's Day" in 1954, it is now celebrated on the fourth Monday in October.
9	alcoholic insanity	The name commonly used prior to the mid - 20th century for the illness of alcoholism. Six forms of the insanity are: 1) delirium tremens 2) alcoholic mania (neurotic character) 3) mania of exhaltation (grandiosity) 4) acute transitary mania (violent or foolish conduct in a blackout) 5) alcoholic dementia (wet brain) 6) dipsomania (periodic alcoholic- a "profound change in moral character" when drinking)
9	two men	Rowland H. (also spelled "Roland"), sober in 1932, and Cebra G. Both were members of the New York Oxford Group.

PEOPLE PLACES AND THINGS

page	reference	people places and things
13	delirium tremens	First named, described and classified as a clinical entity by Dr. Thomas Sutton in 1813.
13	not had a drink since	Bill Wilson's sobriety date is December 11, 1934. He was 39 years old.
15	one western city	Cleveland, Ohio.
16	One poor chap	Bill C., a lawyer.
16	committed suicide	in the summer of 1936.
17	in my home	182 clinton Street, Brooklyn Heights, New York (owned by Dr. Clark & Mrs Burnham).
26	American business man	Rowland H.
28	extraordinary experience	1932
43	staff member	Dr. Percy Polick, a psychiatrist.
43	world renowned hospital	Bellevue Hospital, New York.
50	American Statesman	Alfred E."Al" Smith, four time Governor of New York and unsuccessful first Roman Catholic Presidential candidate in 1928.
51	Galileo	Galileo Galilei (1564-1642) was an Italian astronomer and physicist. He is credited with the formulation of the Law of Falling Bodies. For that discovery, Galileo met with bitter resistance because

PEOPLE PLACES AND THINGS

page	reference	people places and things
		he contradicted the theory of Aristotle and was therefore forced to leave his university post. The Church also bitterly opposed his discoveries in astronomy. He appeared before the Inquisition, was forced to recant his belief in the Copernican theory that the earth revolves around the sun, and was placed under house arrest until his death.
51	Wright brothers	Orville (1871-1948) and Wilbur (1867-1912) Wright. First powered air flight at Kittyhawk, North Carolina in 1904.
55	experience of a man	Fitz M. He was author of the story "Our Southern Friend" in the 1st, 2nd and 3rd editions.
96	one of our fellowship	Bill Wilson.
97	We seldom allow	Bill W. is referring to the experience with Bill C. who lived with them for over a year. See the page 16 reference "One poor chap".
136	I was at one time...	Henry P. He was author of the story: "The Unbeliever" in the 1st edition.

page	reference	people places and things
139	teetotaler	A person who abstains from all alcoholic beverages. Origin of this word is claimed by both England and the U.S. In England, it was purportedly coined by Richard Turner (1790 - 1846) during a speech given in Sept., 1833 which advocated total abstinance from liquor. In the U.S. their are rival derivations. One results from a total abstinence pledge that was promoted as early as 1818 by a temperance society in Hector, NY. In the other derivation the word is credited to Rev. Jewell of the temperance society in Lansing, NY. In a in 1827, he handed out the old temperance pledge cards and encouraged the to sign their names for total abstinance. The members were listed on the rolls as "O.P. - Old Pledge" or "T - Total". The latter were soon known as teetotalers.
140	doctor in Chicago	Dan Craske, M.D. An additional reference is found on page 294: "The doctor, a young man...".
149	little company	Honest Dealers Co. was an automobile polish distributorship. See also page 246.

PEOPLE PLACES AND THINGS

page	reference	people places and things
150	two...employees	Jim B. author of the story "The Vicious Cycle" in the 1st, 2nd and 3rd editions and Bill W.
153	certain western city	Akron, Ohio.
154	hotel lobby	The Mayflower Hotel, 263 South Main Streeet in Akron, Ohio. It is now known as the Mayflower Manor Apartments.
154	clergyman	Rev. Walter F. Tunks, Rector of St. Paul's Episcopal Church, 2896 Hastings Rd., Cuyahoga Falls, Ohio (the church is now located at 1361 West Market Street in Akron Ohio).
155	certain resident	Robert Holbrook Smith, M.D. He was author of the story: "The Doctor's Nightmare" in the 1st edition. The story retitled as: "Dr. Bob's Nightmare" in the 2nd and 3rd editions.
155	his home	855 Ardmore Avenue in Akron, Ohio. The house was designated as a national historical landmark on November 5, 1985.
f155	Bill's first visit	Sunday, May 12, 1935
156	not had a drink since	Dr. Bob's sobriety date is June 10, 1935. He was 55 years old. June 10th is defined as the birth of Alcoholics Anonymous and this date is known as "Founders Day".

page	reference	people places and things
156	head nurse	Mrs. Hall, admissions nurse.
156	local hospital	Akron City Hospital, Akron, Ohio.
156	alcoholic prospect	Bill D., a lawyer. He was the author of the story: "Alcoholics Anonymous Number Three" in the 2nd and 3rd editions.
158	June, 1935	Bill D's sobriety date is June 26, 1935.
158	devil-may-care young fellow	Ernie G. ("the 1st"). He was the author of the story: "The Seven Month Slip" in the 1st edition. He was 30 years old.
160	man and his wife	T. Henry and Clarace Williams. Both were members of the Akron Oxford Group
160	their home	676 Palisades Drive, Akron, Ohio.
161	a community	Cleveland, Ohio.
162	well-known hospital	Charles B. Towns Hospital
162	one of our number	Bill Wilson.
162	this doctor	William D. Silkworth, M.D.
163	an A.A. member	Henry P. See notes to the page 136 reference of "I was at one time..."
163	large community	Montclair, N.J.
163	prominent psychiatrist	Dr. Howard of Montclair, New Jersey.

PEOPLE PLACES AND THINGS

page	reference	people places and things
163	arrangemen	by Bob & Mag V.
163	the chief psychiatrist	Dr. Russell E. Blaisdell.
163	large public hospital	Rockland State Hospital in Rockland County near Orangeburg, New York.

Notes and Remarks

Notes and Remarks

Notes and Remarks

Notes and Remarks

Notes and Remarks

Notes and Remarks

Notes and Remarks

Notes and Remarks

Inquiries, orders, and catalog requests
should be addressed to:

Glen Abbey Books, Inc.
P.O. Box 31329
Seattle, Washington 98103
Call toll-free (all U.S.) 1-800-782-2239